A Guide To
Project Monitoring
&
Evaluation

A Guide To Project Monitoring & Evaluation

Patrick Gudda

authorHOUSE®

AuthorHouse™
1663 Liberty Drive
Bloomington, IN 47403
www.authorhouse.com
Phone: 1-800-839-8640

First published by AuthorHouse   10/27/2011

ISBN: 978-1-4567-8478-2 (sc)
ISBN: 978-1-4567-8479-9 (hc)
ISBN: 978-1-4567-8480-5 (ebk)

Printed in the United States of America

CONTENTS

5. **Program logic:** Is the sequence of planned activities likely to increase the number of years girls stay in school? (Assesses whether the design has correct causal sequence.)

6. **Implementation or process**: Was a project, program, or policy to improve the quality of water supplies in an urban area implemented as intended? (Addresses whether implementation occurred as planned.)

7. **Performance:** Are the planned outcomes and impacts from a policy being achieved? (Establishes links between inputs, activities, outputs, outcomes, and impacts.)

8. **Appropriate use of policy tools**: Has the government made use of the right policy tool in providing subsidies to indigenous farmers to deploy a new agricultural technology? (Establishes whether the appropriate instruments were selected to achieve aims.)

Purpose of the Process

The Project Monitoring and Controlling Processes are used by project managers and project teams to ensure the team is making satisfactory progress to the project goals. The purpose is to track all major project variables—cost, time, scope, and quality of deliverables. The overall objectives of the process are to:

• Track and review actual project accomplishments and results to project plans

• Revise the project plan to reflect accomplishments thus far, and to revise the plan for remaining work, if needed

• Provide visibility into progress as the project proceeds, so that the team and management can take corrective action early when project performance varies significantly from original plans

Deliverables from monitoring and controlling include

- Written status reports
- Updates to lists of action items, risks, problems, and issues
- Updates to the plan and schedule, to reflect actual progress
- Comparisons of actual costs to budgeted costs, as well as the cost/benefit analysis used when starting the project
- Audit and review reports of the activities and work products under development

Principles of Monitoring Systems

Balzer, Dimalanta and Kunz (2004) aver that there is no universally applicable monitoring model. Rather, the scope of a monitoring system is defined by

- The units receiving and using monitoring information and
- The type of information provided

Furthermore, they hold that any monitoring system has to be tailored to the:

- Type, complexity and size of programme
- Institutional set-up
- Managerial responsibilities
- Reporting requirements and dates
- Frame conditions

Monitoring systems must take into account existing rules and procedures for data collection and reporting. Finally, monitoring should allow adjustment of program implementation at the appropriate level and through the responsible personnel.

Framework for Project Monitoring and Evaluation

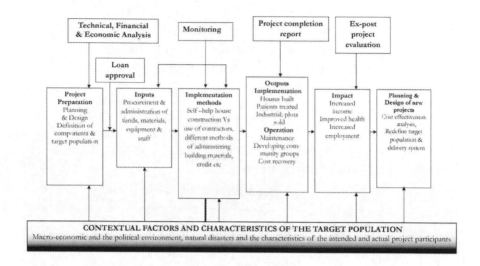

Figure 1-1 is a framework for project monitoring and evaluation. Adapted from the World Bank technical paper: Monitoring and Evaluating Urban Development Programs: A Handbook for Program Managers and Researchers. It breaks down the process into several levels of evaluation.

`1.2 Good Monitoring and Evaluation Design

Good monitoring and evaluation design during project preparation is a much broader exercise than just the development of indicators. Good design has five components:

1. Clear statements of **measurable objectives** for the project and its components, for which indicators can be defined.
2. *A structured set of indicators,* covering outputs of goods and services generated by the project and their impact on beneficiaries.

3. ***Provisions for collecting data and managing project records*** so that the data required for indicators are compatible with existing statistics, and are available at reasonable cost.
4. ***Institutional arrangements for gathering, analyzing, and reporting project data, and for investing in capacity building,*** to sustain the Monitoring and evaluation service.
5. ***Proposals for the ways in which Monitoring and evaluation findings will be fed back into decision making.***

Project Objectives

Projects are designed to further long-term sectoral goals, but their immediate objectives, at least, should be readily measurable (Jiggins, 1995). Thus, for example, a health project might be designed to further the sectoral goals of a reduction in child mortality and incidence of infectious diseases, but have an immediate, measurable objective of providing more equitable access to health services. Objectives should be specific to the project interventions, realistic in the timeframe for their implementation, and measurable for evaluation.

Projects are evaluated with regard to the achievement of the stated outputs as a function of allocated time and resources.

- **'Outputs'** refers to tangible products resulting from a development project, for example, a health facility or a number of houses.
- 'Outcomes' are what the project hopes to achieve as result of the outputs: for example, Capacity Building and Empowerment.

Thurwa's District Primary Education Project, for example, set out its objectives at the district level in clear statements linked directly to indicators: Capacity building: District sub-project teams would be fully functional, implementing sub-project activities and reporting quarterly on progress. In-service teams would be functioning, with augmented staff and equipment, providing support for planning and management, teacher in-service training, development of learning materials, and program evaluation. Reducing dropout and improving learning achievement: School/community organizations would be fully functional for at least half the schools, and dropout rates would be reduced to less than 10 percent. Learning achievements in language and mathematics in the final year of primary school would be increased by 25 percent over baseline estimates. Improving equitable access. Enrollment disparities by gender and caste would be reduced to less than five percent.

INDICATORS

Indicators are measures of change(s) brought about by an activity. Indicators communicate information about progress towards particular goals, provide clues about matters of larger significance, or make perceptible a trend or a phenomenon that is not immediately detectable (Hammond *et al*, 1995). The indicators provide both qualitative and quantitative data that reveal the effectiveness of project implementation that is, problems encountered and successes achieved so far. Indicators can be used for many purposes, such as:

- Providing a framework for collecting and reporting information;
- Providing guidance to various organizations on needs, priorities and policy effectiveness; and
- Facilitating local community efforts to undertake and strengthen development plans.

The choice of indicators depends on the purpose for which they are required and on the audience. Formative indicators are set with a time frame to be measured during a phase or project and are the same as milestones. Summative indicators are used to measure performance at the end. It is worth noting that indicators should be specific, verifiable, logical and cost-effective.

i) ***Specific and measurable:***—in terms of quality, quantity, time, location and target group.
ii) ***Relevant and substantial:***—they need to catch the core of a particular objective.
iii) ***Sensitive:***—show changes in short, medium or long-term that will be happening as a result of the project / programme.
iv) ***Cost-effective:***—can be measured with reasonable cost and effort, proportionate with the scale of the project / programme.
v) ***Verifiable and available:***—the information needs to be collected at the time planned. When deciding on means of verification
   • Describe the data needed;
   • Source of primary / secondary data;
   • Who will collect and document the data and
   • The frequency and dates of data collection.
vi) ***Logical:***—the objectives and their indicators need to be necessary and sufficient to achieve wider objectives.

The "CREAM" of Good Performance Indicators

The "CREAM" of selecting good performance indicators is essentially a set of criteria to aid in developing indicators for a specific project, program, or policy (Schiavo-Campo 1999, p. 85). Performance indicators should be clear, relevant, economic, adequate, and monitorable. CREAM amounts to an insurance policy, because the more precise and coherent the indicators, the better focused the measurement strategies will be.

Clear:—Precise and unambiguous

Relevant:—Appropriate to the subject at hand
Economic:—Available at a reasonable cost
Adequate;—Provide a sufficient basis to assess performance
Monitorable:—Amenable to independent validation

If any one of these five criteria is not met, formal performance indicators will suffer and be less useful. Performance indicators should be as clear, direct, and unambiguous as possible.

The following are examples of indicators at various levels. The table below provides an example of an outcome and some possible program and project level indicators.

Program and Project Level Results Indicators: An Example from the Irrigation Sector

Level		Result
Project name		Strengthening irrigation in a specific country area
Project goals		Improve agricultural productivity
		Raise farm income
Indicators	Outcome indicators	New area under irrigation
		Higher yield
		Increased production
		Increased farm income.
	Output indicators	Construction of 10 new irrigation schemes
		Reconstruction of five old irrigation schemes
		Twenty-five farmer training sessions.

Source: Adapted from IFAD 2002, p.19.

As proposed by Kusek and Rist (2004), there are eight key questions that should be asked in building baseline information for every indicator. (These questions continue to apply in subsequent efforts to measure the indicator.)

1. What are the sources of data? Sources are who or what provide data—not the method of collecting data.
2. What are the data collection methods?

Informal and less-structured methods

- o Conversation with concerned individuals
- o Field visits
- o Reviews of official records (management information system and administrative data)
- o Key informant interviews
- o Participant observation
- o Focus group interviews

Formal and more-structured methods

- o Direct observation
- o Questionnaires
- o One-time survey
- o Panel surveys
- o Census
- o Field experiments
- o Community interviews

3. Who will collect the data?
4. How often will the data be collected?
5. What is the cost and difficulty to collect the data?

Data collection strategies necessarily involve some tradeoffs with respect to cost, precision, credibility, and timeliness. For example, the more structured and formal methods for collecting data generally tend to be more precise, costly, and time consuming. If data are needed frequently and on a routine basis to inform management decision-making, it may be preferable to adopt less precise, more unstructured, and inexpensive data collection strategies.

After gathering baseline data on indicators, the next step is to establish results targets—what can be achieved in a specific time toward reaching the outcome. Identifying the expected and desired level of project, program, or policy results requires the selection of specific performance targets. Target setting is the final step in building the performance framework. It, in turn, is based on outcomes, indicators, and baselines. The reasoning process is a deductive one, flowing back from the desired outcomes.

A **target** is " . . . a specified objective that indicates the number, timing and location of that which is to be realized" (IFAD 2002, p. 11). Kusek and. Rist (2004) hold that targets are interim stepson the way to an outcome and eventually to a longer-term goal. In essence, targets are the quantifiable levels of the indicators that a country, society, or organization wants to achieve by a given time. Targets are based on known resources (financial and organizational) plus a reasonable projection of the available resource base over a fixed period of time

Characteristic	Review of program records	Self-administered questionnaire	Interview	Rating by trained observer
Cost	Low	high	Moderate to high	Depends on Availability of low cost observers
Amount of training required to high for data collectors	Some	none to some	Moderate to high	Moderate to high
Completion time	Depends on amount of data needed	Moderate	Moderate	Short to moderate
Response rate	High, if records contains needed data	Depends on how distributed	Generally moderate to good	High

Source: Adapted from Kusek & Rist (2004) *Ten Steps to a Results—Based Monitoring and Evaluation System: A Handbook f o r D e v e l o p m e n t P r a c t i t i o n e r s Washington*, **D.C.** The International Bank for Reconstruction and Development / The World Bank p.87

6. Who will analyze the data?
7. Who will report the data?
8. Who will use the data?

Indicators range from primary, secondary, direct, indirect to quantitative and qualitative indicators. *Primary indicators:* can be measured directly e.g. except (sales vol., no of personnel trained etc). *Secondary indicators*: are relative measures derived from primary indicators. The indicators would focus on:

i) **Relevance:**—does the project / programme address the needs?
ii) **Efficiency:**—are we using the available resources wisely?

18

iii) **Effectiveness:**—are the desired outputs being achieved? Is the project delivering results it set out with?

iv) **Impact:**—have wider goals been achieved? What changes have occurred that help targeted individuals and or communities?

v) **Sustainability:**—will the impact be sustainable? Will any structures and processes established be sustained?

Input indicators are quantified and time-bound statements of resources to be provided. Information on these indicators comes largely from accounting and management records. Input indicators are often left out of discussions of project monitoring, though they are part of the management information system. A good accounting system is needed to keep track of expenditures and provide cost data for performance analysis of outputs. Input indicators are used mainly by managers closest to the tasks of implementation, and are consulted frequently, as often as daily or weekly.

Process indicators measure what happens during implementation. Often, they are tabulated as a set of contracted completions or milestone events taken from an activity plan. There are a great many 'process' issues, which might be measured in connection with projects, all leading to increased capacities and self-reliance. According to Meyer and Singh (2003) four process indicators are identified below:

i.   Capacity building on the part of the individuals or local group in a community. Guiding questions would include: what new skills have been acquired? What local knowledge has been identified and used? What institutions have been strengthened?

ii. Organizational skills suggest the development of group capabilities in identifying problems, prioritizing solutions, implementing programmes, dealing with conflict, consensus building, negotiation and problem solving.

iii. Leadership is an essential element in strengthening local communities. The emergence of local leadership committed to these goals and able to mobilize and organize local groups is an important part of this process.

iv. Partnerships can strengthen development effort through linking the various stakeholders in a common effort. Partnerships that build relationships between local communities and external agents, regional, national, and even international can help bring a project to fruition and can serve as an indicator that the project is not likely to wither in isolation and neglect.

Examples: Date by which building site clearance must be completed; latest date for delivery of fertilizer to farm stores; number of health outlets reporting family planning activity; number of women receiving contraceptive counseling; status of procurement of school textbooks.

Output indicators show the immediate physical and financial outputs of the project in terms of physical quantities, organizational strengthening, and initial flows of services. They include performance measures based on cost or operational ratios.

Examples: Kilometers of all-weather highway completed by the end of September; percentage of farmers attending a crop demonstration site before fertilizer top-dressing; number of teachers trained in textbook use; cost per kilometer of road construction; crop yield per hectare; ratio of textbooks to pupils; time taken to process a credit application; number of demonstrations managed per extension worker; steps in the process of establishing water users' associations.

The Use of Proxy Indicators

You may not always be precise with indicators, but you can strive to be approximately right. Sometimes it is difficult to measure the outcome indicator directly, so proxy indicators are needed. According to Kusek and Rist (2004) indirect, or proxy, indicators should be used only when data for direct indicators are not available, when data collection will be too costly, or if it is not feasible to collect data at regular intervals. However, caution should be exercised in using proxy indicators, because there has to be a presumption that the proxy indicator is giving at least approximate evidence on performance. For example, if it is difficult to conduct periodic household surveys in dangerous housing areas, one could use the number of tin roofs or television antennas as a proxy measure of increased household in—come. These proxy indicators might be correctly tracking the desired outcome, but there could be other contributing factors as well; for example, the increase in income could be attributable to drug money, or income generated from the hidden market, or recent electrification that now allows the purchase of televisions. These factors would make attribution to the policy or program of economic development more difficult to assert.

Impact refers to medium or long-term developmental change. (Some writers also refer to a further class of outcome indicators, more specific to project activities than impact indicators, which may be sectoral statistics, and deal more with the direct effect of project outputs on beneficiaries). Measures of change often involve complex statistics about economic or social welfare and depend on data that are gathered from beneficiaries (Kezsbom, Donald, and Katherine (1989). Early indications of impact may be obtained by surveying beneficiaries' perceptions about project services. This type of leading indicator has the twin benefits of consultation with stakeholders and advance warning of problems that might arise.

IMPACT INDICATORS HAVE BOTH QUALITATIVE AND QUANTITATIVE DIMENSIONS.

i.   Productivity:—can be measured in terms of increased output per given unit of land, labour, or period of time. Improved productivity may also be a matter of decreased labour time for the same output and it cam be determined by measuring income.

ii. Welfare:—has many dimensions. It should be possible to select those most relevant to the type of project e.g. health, educational opportunity, nutrition, improved housing, better sanitation.

iii. Equity:—as a measure will suggest how broadly based are improvements in welfare and productivity. It requires consideration of social groups and suggests that the contextual analysis (as part of the primary data—gathering exercise) is an important component of building indicators.

iv. Environment:—requires measures of the ways in which a project is affecting soil fertility, water quality and retention, erosion, natural vegetation and biodiversity.

Examples of impact*: (health) incidence of low birth weight, percentage of women who are moderately or severely anemic; (education) continuation rates from primary to secondary education by sex, proportion of girls completing secondary education; (forestry) percent decrease in area harvested, percent increase in household income through sales of wood and non-wood products. Examples of beneficiary perceptions: proportion of farmers who have tried a new variety of seed and intend to use it again; percentage of women satisfied with the maternity health care they receive.

Sustainability Indicators are essential for determining not only the viability of the project at the moment the evaluation is being prepared, but also its longevity and influence. Four indicators are identified below.

    i.   Replicability suggests that others can readily undertake a similar project. If there is spontaneous replication, so much the better. This implies that the project is spreading on the basis of its own merits without an outside organizer or initiator.

    ii. Local ownership is an important indicator of the project's lifetime. If local people find it useful, want it to continue and are prepared to assume responsibility for assuring the continuation, local ownership has been achieved and so is the level of local empowerment.

    iii. Cost-effectiveness is an essential part of sustainability, although it may be difficult to separate from the impact indicators. If the project is not cost-effective—in the broadest sense of the term, including all levels of effort required of the local people to sustain it is then unlikely to be supported by the local residents. Three types of cost-effectiveness, each designed to meet the needs of different kinds of projects, include:
- Measures of costs in comparison with community resources;
- The ratio of net benefits to costs; and
- The ratio of per-unit costs.

Environmental sustainability is an essential element of sustainability. If the project or programme has, on balance, a negative impact on its environment, it may bring short-term benefits (such as some types of mining) but is not sustainable in the long-term. Many projects have both positive and negative effects on the environment, and these must be weighed in each situation.

The Table below clarifies how the indicators connect the enabling conditions revealing the latter's relevance to meeting environmental and economic objectives in various projects.

limited number of key indicators needed to summarize overall progress in reports to higher management levels.

For example, during construction of village tube wells, project managers will need to keep records about the materials purchased and consumed, the labor force employed and their contracting details, the specific screen and pump fitted, the depth at which water was found, and the flow rate. The key indicators however, might be just the number of wells successfully completed and their average costs and flow rates.

Exogenous indicators are those that cover factors outside the control of the project but which might affect its outcome, including risks (parameters identified during economic, social, or technical analysis, that might compromise project benefits); and the performance of the sector in which the project operates. Concerns to monitor both the project and its wider environment call for a data collection capacity outside the project and place an additional burden on the project's Monitoring and evaluation effort. An example of a grain storage project in Myanmar demonstrates the importance of monitoring risk indicators. During project implementation, policy decisions about currency exchange rates and direct access by privately owned rice mills to overseas buyers adversely affected the profitability of private mills. Management would have been alerted to the deteriorating situation had these indicators of the enabling environment been carefully monitored. Instead, a narrow focus on input and process indicators missed the fundamental change in the assumptions behind the project. The relative importance of indicators is likely to change during the implementation of a project, with more emphasis on input and process indicators at first, shifting to outputs and impact later on. This is a distinction between indicators of implementation progress and indicators of development results.

Data collection Project field records. Indicators of inputs and processes will come from project management records originating from field sites. The quality of record keeping in the field sets the standard for all further use of the data and merits careful attention. Monitoring and evaluation designers should examine existing record-keeping and the reporting procedures used by the project authorities to assess the capacity to generate the data that will be needed. At the same time, they should explain how and why the indicators will be useful to field, intermediate, and senior levels of project management. The design of field records about, say, farmers in extension groups, people attending a clinic, or villagers using a new water supply, will affect the scope for analysis later. The inclusion of simple socioeconomic characteristics such as age and sex may significantly improve the scope for analysis. A good approach is to structure reporting from the field so that aggregates or summaries are made at intermediate stages. In this way, field staff can see how averages or totals for specific villages or districts enable comparisons to be drawn and fieldwork improved.

Surveys and studies. To measure output and impact may require the collection of data from sample surveys or special studies (including, where appropriate, participatory methods). Studies to investigate specific topics may call for staff skills and training beyond those needed for regular collection of data to create a time series. Where there is a choice, it is usually better to piggyback project-specific regular surveys on to existing national or internationally supported surveys than to create a new data collection facility. Special studies may be more manageable by a project unit directly, or subcontracted to a university or consultants. If the special studies are to make comparisons with data from other surveys it is vital that the same methods be used for data collection (see below). In the project plan, proposals to collect data for studies should include a discussion of: the objectives of the study or survey; the source of data; choices and proposed method of collection; and likely reliability of the data.

Data comparability. Some desired indicators of impact, such as mortality rates, school attendance, or household income attributable to a project, may involve comparisons with the situation before the project, or in areas not covered by the project. Such comparisons may depend on the maintenance of national systems of vital statistics, or to transparent management and good information about progress. The other is that often beneficiaries doubt the value of adopting what may be costly and time consuming procedures to collect, analyze, and report information. In such circumstances sound design is especially important, with monitoring information providing a clear input to management decision making and, often, an emphasis on the early gains to be had from monitoring and on institutional procedures that encourage the use of monitoring data to trigger further implementation decisions.

Using Evaluation Outcomes

Evaluation information can help differentiate between the contributions of design and implementation to outcomes. In the figure below, **Quadrant 1** is the best place to be—the design (a causal model of how to bring about desired change in an existing problem) is strong and the implementation of actions to address the problem is also strong. All managers, planners, and implementers would like to spend their time and efforts like this—making good things happen for which there is demonstrable evidence of positive change.

	Strength of Design	
	High	**Low**
Reliability High	1	2
Low	3	4

Quadrant 2 generates considerable ambiguity in terms of performance on outcome indicators. In this situation there is a weak design that is strongly implemented—but with little to no evident results. The evidence suggests successful implementation, but few results. The evaluative questions would turn to the strength and logic of the design. For example, was the causal model appropriate? Was it sufficiently robust that, if implemented well, it would bring about the desired change? Was the problem well understood and clearly defined? Did the proposed change strategy directly target the causes of the problem?

Quadrant 3 also generates considerable ambiguity in terms of performance with respect to outcome indicators. In this situation there is a well-crafted design that is poorly implemented—again, with little to no evident results. This is the reverse situation of Quadrant 2, but with the same essential outcome—no clear results. The evaluative questions focus on the implementation processes and procedures: Did what was supposed to take place actually take place? When, and in what sequence? With what level of support? With what expertise among the staff? The emphasis is on trying to learn what happened during implementation that brought down and rendered ineffective a potentially successful policy, program, or project.

Quadrant 4 is not a good place to be. A weak design that is badly implemented leaves only the debris of good intentions. There will be no evidence of outcomes. The evaluation information can document both the weak design and the poor implementation. The challenge for the manager is to figure out how to close down this effort quickly so as to not prolong its ineffectiveness and negative consequences for all involved.

Field Visits

Programme or project managers must make field visits at regular intervals and adequate budgetary resources should be allocated for this purpose. In addition to inspecting the sites, physical outputs and services of the programme or project, the visits must focus on interaction with target groups to obtain their views on how the programme or project is affecting them (directly or indirectly, positively or negatively) and their proposed solutions to perceived problems.

Persons undertaking the field visits must prepare their reports either at the site or immediately after the visits, focusing on relevance and performance, including early signs of potential problem or success areas

Stakeholder Meetings

The objective of stakeholder meetings is to involve the major stakeholders in addressing issues that pertain to the programmes or projects, thereby creating a sense of ownership. The Government (for Government funded projects) plays a key role in identifying the stakeholders. Besides the executing and implementing agencies and other development partners, it is essential that target groups that are expected to be affected by the programmes or projects be involved in the discussion of issues relevant to them.

Depending on the issues and problems to be addressed, these meetings may be conducted at different levels and venues with varying frequency. Technical and operational issues may be handled at the programme or project management level whereas policy issues that have significant implications for the programme or project and their ultimate beneficiaries may be discussed at a higher level, e.g., bipartite or tripartite reviews.

Programme or project management meetings must be conducted regularly. Bipartite or tripartite meetings must be held once a year, with additional meetings if the need arises. Reports should be prepared on all of these meetings

Systematic Reporting during Implementation

There must be systematic reporting on all programmes and projects regardless of budget or duration. The executing agency must submit an annual report to on the relevance, performance and likelihood of success of the programme or project.

Internally, however, the programme or project management must prepare monitoring reports more frequently (i.e., monthly, quarterly and/or semi-annually) to serve its internal management requirements.

Terminal Reports

Upon completion of a programme or project, the executing agency must prepare a terminal report that focuses on the relevance and performance of the programme or project, the likelihood of its success, and the initial lessons learned in terms of best and worst practices. The report should also contain recommendations for follow-up actions by appropriate institutions where necessary.

Other ways of project monitoring

There are four other ways to monitor:

i) *Briefing;*—each and every stakeholder needs to know the objectives, what is required of them.
ii) *Project charts:*—gives timing and schedules of the various activities. It enables us identify whether we are lagging behind or ahead of time or problems that are being experienced

iii) Surprise /visits:—makes everyone involved and is committed to their tasks.

iv) Morning prayers (departmental/section heads):—the project team should meet at least once a week and exchange views on ideas, progress, problems experienced and thereafter put in place mitigation plans.

MONITORING TOOLS

The monitoring tools include:

a) *Project breakdown structure (PBS)*—it involves breaking down the project into a hierarchical structure of its component parts. It enables the project officer to identify relationships between the various parts and start to visualize the sequence in which different tasks should be carried out. The PBS does not deal explicitly with time but it often expresses an input to more complex monitoring instruments.

b) *Gantt charts:*—provide a graphical representation of the project related to a time frame.

c) *Milestone charts:*—is a development of a bar chart. Milestones or check points, representing key events in time are introduced into the chart. These are used as reference points when reporting on progress with specific activities / the exercise as a whole.

d) *Network instruments* (CPA and PERT).

PROJECT (RE) DESIGN

Project (re)design is an ongoing process throughout the life of the project, managers and implementing partners must understand the principles of good design to be able to adapt project strategy and operations in response to changing circumstances and lessons of implementation experience. The key messages here are:

Good practices for project design (and redesign/adoption) include:

- Involving stakeholders;
- Completing a detailed situation analysis;
- Ensuring a logical intervention strategy;
- Identifying cross-cutting objectives;
- Planning for capacity development and sustainability; and
- Planning for learning and adaptation.

The logical framework approach is a valuable tool for project design provided it is used in a flexible manner and its common problems are understood and addressed. The logical framework matrix summarizes a project's intervention logic, its underlying assumptions and how Monitoring and evaluation will be undertaken. The matrix constitutes a useful management tool and forms the basis for operational and annual work plans, but consistent and regular use and attention to detail are needed.

Developing a good Monitoring and evaluation system calls for adequate attention to Monitoring and evaluation during the initial design phase. The Monitoring and evaluation system should be outlined in the project appraisal report.

PARTICIPATORY MONITORING

Participatory Monitoring continuously tracks performance against what was planned by collecting and analyzing data on the indicators established for monitoring and evaluation purposes. It provides continuous information on whether progress is being made toward achieving results (outputs, outcomes, and goals) through record keeping and regular reporting systems. Monitoring looks at both programme processes and changes in conditions of target groups and institutions brought about by programme activities. It also identifies strengths and weaknesses in a programme. The performance information generated from monitoring enhances learning from experience and improves decision-making. Management and programme implementers typically conduct monitoring.

Participatory monitoring involves the target group(s) in the collection and assessment of Monitoring information as well as in the discussion of corrective measures. Benefits that accrue from participatory monitoring include:

- Increases the target groups′ awareness and understanding of development and their ability to control this process
- Improves the understanding of the role of the project for the target group(s)
- (Often) improves the quality of the Monitoring data / information

Characteristics of participatory monitoring

- Objectives, Indicators and sources of verification are defined in close collaboration between target group(s) and project team
- Target group(s) assess the situation and analyze monitoring data with "outsiders from the project" acting as facilitators
- Feed back to the target group(s) is immediate and becomes the basis for self-induced reflections and decision making
- Self assessment skills are developed within target group(s)

STEPS TO PARTICIPATORY MONITORING TECHNIQUES

1) Focus on objectives of the monitoring system
2) Selection of relevant information and determination of indicators.
3) Identification of methods and tools for data collection.
4) Analyze data and interpret results generated.
5) Presentation of the information
6) Provide recommendations to the various stakeholders.
7) Maintaining monitoring systems.

The adoption of Results-based Management provides an opportunity to explore different approaches and methods which involve stakeholders more directly in building sustainable development results through their active participation in all dimensions of the project cycle.

What is the difference between conventional monitoring and evaluation and Results-based Participatory Monitoring and Evaluation?

Some differences		
	Conventional	**Participatory Monitoring and Evaluation**
Who initiates?	Donor	The donor and project stakeholders
Purpose	Donor accountability	Capacity building increases ownership over results, multi-stakeholder accountability
Who evaluates?	*External evaluator*	*Project stakeholders assisted by PM& E facilitator*
TOR	Designed by Donor	with limited input
Methods	Survey, Questionnaire,	Range of methods such as Participatory
	Semi-structured Interviewing,	Learning and Action, Appreciative Inquiry,
	Focus Groups.	Testimonials.

Outcome	Final report circulated in-house.	Better understanding of local realities, stakeholders involved in decision-making around analysis and what to do with information to adjust project strategies and activities to better

THE PURPOSE OF PM&E

The purpose of PM&E is fourfold:

1) to build local capacity of project stakeholders to reflect, analyze, propose solutions and take action;
2) to learn, adjust and take action by taking corrective action to ensure the achievement of results such as adding or deleting activities or changing one's strategies;
3) To provide accountability at all levels from the community, organizational level to those responsible for the implementation and funding of the project.
4) To celebrate and build on what is working.

Stakeholders are involved in defining what will be evaluated, who will be involved, when it will take place, the participatory methods for collecting information and analysis to be used and how findings are consolidated. Random sampling and triangulation are integral to PM&E to ensure that the findings are valid and reliable.

Stakeholders drawn from the project may need to be trained to act as PM&E facilitators. Learning, proposing solutions and acting on them are also an important part of participation, learning and action.

KEY PRINCIPLES OF PM&E

Principles of PM&E Include

- Letting go of your own preconceived ideas and viewpoints;
- The importance of "handing over the stick" and creating the space for respect and participation;
- PM&E should not be an extractive process of information gathering;
- PM&E leads to reflection on the achievement of results in order to effect positive and constructive change;
- Respecting local customs, languages and experiences;
- Believing in and seeking the knowledge that marginalized or illiterate people have of their environment;
- Facilitating a process of learning, change and action versus prescribing, judging or punishing;
- Living with the people and integrating oneself with local customs and traditions;
- People will open-up if they are allowed to participate;
- Emphasizing listening skills and rapport-building;
- Flexibility to adjust approach and strategies.

Salient features of PM&E include:

1. The PM&E framework for a project should be simple, affordable and sustainable given the human and financial resources available. One should resist creating a monster or a system that is too complex or unwieldy.
2. PM&E tools are not an end onto itself, but a vehicle for group discussion, analysis, problem-solving and action.
3. PM&E should seek to give voice to local needs, priorities, aspirations and resources.
4. PM&E builds on the participatory creation of expected results.

5. The framework and its implementation should complement existing monitoring and evaluation efforts.

6. PM&E relies on local resources and materials and uses such techniques to monitor results as semi-structured interviewing, stakeholder analysis, mapping, trend analysis, drawings, flowcharts, collection of baseline, etc.

7. PM&E is more than training; it is a process that is on going and continuous involving a framework for action rather than a one-off activity.

8. PM&E should emphasize a positive approach to learning and improving performance recognizing commitment, innovation and flexibility versus judgment or punishment.

9. Emphasis should be on action and taking the learning to achieve meaningful development results versus simply collecting information. Conventional

Ideally, PM&E should be an integral part of a project from the early design and planning stage. PM&E is best integrated during the first year of operation so that the PM&E needs can be identified, baseline established and capacity built from the onset. Where projects are already on going, one must discuss with the project stakeholders their interest and desire to integrate PM&E. PM&E undertaken in traditionally designed projects may help a project to identify and integrate more participatory methods in their project management.

Remember that increased investments in PM&E can be offset by long-term benefits. PM&E and Participatory RBM strengthens local capacity in participatory planning and decision-making processes.

CRITICAL SUCCESS FACTORS OF PM&E

Coupal (2001) identifies at least six key phases to PM&E and a number of key steps for each phase. These are:

Phase 1: Buy-in and Commitment

- Find out what is being monitored and evaluated already and what methods and approaches are being used;
- Explore people's understanding of participation and to what degree they can and want to participate in the monitoring and evaluation of their project.
- Introduce the idea of PM&E to those who are unfamiliar with it.
- If buy-in and commitment to PM&E exists, proceed to identify those to be involved in the first steps such as "beneficiaries", community representatives, intermediaries such as NGOs and even the donor.
- Identify the information needs of each stakeholder group that needs to be met by the M&E process;
- Agree on how each of the stakeholder groups will/wishes/can be involved;
- Reflect on and improve the PM&E process, based on what has been done so far.

Phase 2: Training in PM&E Methods

- Start small by piloting PM&E in one region before trying to cover too much;
- Train all relevant people (i.e. beneficiaries, community leaders, intermediaries, technical M&E staff, executing agency) in PM&E methods and approaches;
- Ensure that community leaders are part of the capacity building and that there is a good gender mix;

- Include a field practice with the training with participants residing in the community for a few days;
- Reflect on and improve the PM&E process, based on what has been done so far.

Determining the Costs

1. *Take stock of existing resources both human and professional;*
2. *Start small, piloting PM&E in one region;*
3. *Determine counterpart contribution;*
4. *Identify capacity of local stakeholders for undertaking PM&E;*
5. *Determine the need for hiring a PM&E facilitator experienced in PM&E methods;*

Phase 3: Defining a Framework for PM&E

- Establish the level (i.e. village, township, regional or organizational level) PM&E is to operate. Keep it simple and pilot PM&E in a given region before expanding;
- Clarify the objectives, results (short, medium and long-term results) and any on-going activities to be monitored and evaluated;
- Decide how you are going to monitor the PM&E process itself;
- Plan how you will prioritize what to monitor and evaluate; define the most appropriate indicators, the sources of information, the methods to be used and who will be responsible;
- Clarify the rights and responsibilities of each stakeholder in the PM&E process;
- Define a locally based PM&E team that will be responsible for the PM&E;
- Determine the need for the use of specialized software for tabulating data;

- Reflect on and improve the PM&E process, based on what has been done so far.

Phase 4: Implementing PM&E

- Organize logistics with communities and organizations beforehand and ensure that the timing and purpose is clear and agreeable;
- If the PM&E team is large, break down into small teams of three-four persons each to cover various communities effectively;
- Ensure your sample is representative;
- Reflect on and improve the PM&E process, based on what has been done so far.

Phase 5: Data Collection, Participatory Analysis and Action

- Collect and analyze the information with the communities with the application of PM&E tools and methods;
- Brainstorm possible solutions and actions with the community or organization that is part of the PM&E process;
- Ensure feedback of the findings to the communities through pre-departure debriefings;
- Make decisions with the community about the implications of the analyzed information for the project and the stakeholders;
- Agree on the recommendations for decision-making;
- Determine how findings will be presented (i.e. theatre, presentations, skits, video, or written report);
- Circulate and distribute any documentation arising from the PM&E to meet information needs of the different stakeholders. Always ensure that all stakeholders have copies of the information down to the grassroots level. Translation may be required.

- Reflect on and improve the PM&E process, based on what has been done so far.

Phase 6: Next Steps

- Determine next steps with key project stakeholders such as piloting in other regions, scaling up, creating local capacity for analysis and action;
- Follow-up recommendations and proposals to ensure that decision-making is being informed by PM&E findings;
- Ensure that there is project/programme flexibility to incorporate suggested changes;
- Reflect on and improve the PM&E process, based on what has been done so far;
- Celebrate.

There are no standard recipes for undertaking participatory monitoring and evaluation. PM&E involves creating a framework that suits the context of the project and the needs of the key stakeholders. "Just get out there and do it so you can see how different it is than conventional methods". Being aware of the advantages of PM&E, creating space for the experimentation of PM&E methods during field visits and piloting initiatives is the first step to greater participation and ownership of project results.

PROJECT AUDIT

The Project Management Body of Knowledge defines project audit as a "structured independent review to determine whether project activities comply with organizational policies and procedures (Project Management Institute, 2004, p. 189). In short, it is a quality management tool.

As the projects become larger and more complex, understanding and providing effective validation of the project management processes is a significant challenge for today's organizations. In addition to the awareness and implementation of the project management procedures, recognition of the quality of the standards and practices is critical for continued performance improvement.

Although recognizing a "failed" project is fairly easy, collecting the lessons learned and translating them into improved project management practices is sometimes performed sporadically or left up to the individual project managers. Once identified, incorporating the most effective practices into an organization's methodologies and obtaining real behavior changes in the overtaxed project manager is even more difficult. Project audits can be used on both the people and process side by serving two major purposes.

Project audits are used to check compliance and ensure that project management processes are being used as they should. Specifically, project audits may be used to:

- Revalidate the business feasibility of the project
- Reassure top management
- Confirm readiness to move to next phase of project
- Investigate specific problems

The results of the project audits will be used as input into the periodic organization assessments.

Auditing can also be an opportunity for coaching. The auditor can act as a coach and assist the project manager in understanding how the methodology is applicable to his or her project. If project managers are open-minded, a project audit can be an opportunity to learn new things about how the project management processes apply to them. If there are areas where the audit finds room for improvement, the project manager and the auditor can discuss the value of the additional recommendations.

Some project managers see project audits as a point of intrusion by the PMO, and a mechanism for slapping them if they are not following the processes as they should. However, if a project manager chooses to take advantage of project audits, they can be great opportunities for learning—since many of the services provided by the PMO, such as coaching and training, are designed to build capability and increase the skill levels of the project team members.

A formal Project Audit program helps ensure project success through independent project assessment and identification of positives and improvement areas.

Objectives

A project audit is performed to provide the client with objective visibility into their application of project management best practices. In addition, specific objectives include:

1. Insight into the project team's use of the project management standards
2. Identification of the project's project management related risks

3. Detail corrective action plan for addressing the risks, incomplete procedures and standards training
4. Awareness of the areas of opportunity for improvement of the project management methods and behaviors

Costs of Project Audits

While audits offer benefits, they aren't free. Some costs are obvious, such as salaries of auditors and staff; others are less obvious such as distraction from project work (before and during the audit); anxiety and morale within the project.

TYPES OF PROJECT AUDITS

To ensure the audit is unbiased, the reviewers should have no conflict of interest and be independent, i.e. not being related to or controlled by the party being audited. Organizations may use a combination of project management office staff, internal audit staff, external auditors and or external third party experts. The audit team should include functional as well as subject matter experts e.g. if the project is information system related, the business viewpoint must be represented as well as information technology. For post implementation audit, some businesses include team members from the project implementation team, but then ensure the audit team lead is independent.

A third party firm may be used when the internal audit function lack bandwidth or expertise in a given subject matter. Some prescient organizations even plan for such possibilities as part of their procurement.

Using predefined standards and best project management practices, an independent experienced auditor reviews the project related documentation, interviews selected project participants, assesses the risks and prepares a formal audit report that documents the findings and identifies the necessary corrective actions. There are **several variations of a project audit**: in-process quality assurance review, project management audit, and post implementation audit.

Gateway audits are conducted at the end of a project phase and prior to progressing to the next phase. A project audit may be conducted at any time but is often timed so that sufficient deliverables are available for review, or when a project sponsor seeks an independent assessment of project success. **Post implementation review** occurs at the end of a project but the exact time could be from a few weeks to a year, depending on what is to be examined. It can be difficult to analyze benefits unless sufficient time has lapsed and the proper benefits realization process has been realized. Ideally, the auditors should be able to examine the already realized benefits measurement procedures and compare initial benchmarks with on-going results.

Project Lifecycle AND management audit

Early audits tend to focus on technical issues, and tend to benefit the **project.** Later audits lean toward cost and schedule, and tend to benefit the parent organization through transfer of lessons learned to other projects. Depending on the project's life cycle, two or more of the following four types of project management audits can be performed.

1. **Pre-Audit**—During project definition phase, ensures the Project Control and Reporting Process (PCRP) standard is incorporated and the project is set up for success by confirming the definition is complete, a risk mitigation plan is in place, the scope is well defined and change will be effectively managed.
2. **Mini-Audit**—Performed periodically throughout the project's execution to ensure it is progressing according to Productivity Management Principles and PCRP standard.

3. **Full Audit**—Performed on request to provide an extensive review of the project and to identify real or potential problems and suggest specific correction actions.
4. **Post Project Audit**—Once the project is complete, provides visibility into what went well during the project and areas for future improvement.

The Benefits

Some benefits of project audits

- Identify problems earlier
- Clarify performance/cost/schedule relationships
- Reconfirm feasibility of/commitment to project
- Independent evaluation of project management performance
- Identification of project management related risks for new or active projects
- Identify future opportunities
- Inform client of project status/prospects
- Specific action plan for each audited project thereby minimizing future deviations

Improved likelihood of project success of the audit methodology is on the processes and guidelines being used to manage projects—not the content and quality of deliverables or the appropriate use of technology. The goal is to identify areas in the management process that work well and areas where adjustments to the process can be recommended for the benefit of future work—not to focus on past mistakes. When done throughout the life of the project, corrective actions to enhance performance in the future on the project will be determined.

The audit deliverables consist of an audit report and presentation of the report to the project team and other client personnel. The "Findings" section of the final report includes roles and responsibilities, project planning and definition, project tracking and control, change control and acceptance, and project communication and reporting.

Participants

For each project audit, the following individuals may be involved:

1. Project manager of audited project
2. Project team representatives
3. Business area project team members
4. Business project sponsor
5. Senior executive
6. Project officer

CONTENTS OF THE PROJECT AUDIT

Format can vary, but six areas should be covered

1. Project status, in all dimensions
2. Future projections
3. Status of crucial tasks
4. Risk assessment
5. Information relevant to other projects
6. Limitations of the audit exercise

A FORMAT FOR A PROJECT AUDIT

- Introduction
    - Including project objectives
    - Also audit assumptions, limitations

- Current project status in terms of cost / schedule / progress/ earned value / quality
  - ° Future Project Status, conclusions and recommendations
- Critical Management Issues by applying a Pareto approach
- Risk Management; identify major threats to project success
  - ° Appendices

THE PROJECT AUDIT LIFE CYCLE

Like the project itself, the audit has a life cycle. It has six basic steps are:

Project audit initiation

- Determine the focus and scope of audit;
- Assess methodologies appropriate for the audit,
- Determine the competencies of team members required

Baseline Definition

- Determine the standards against which performance will be measured

Establishment of Audit Database

- Entails gathering/organizing pertinent data
- Focus on what's necessary

Data Analysis

- This is the judgment stage
- It entails analysis and comparison of actual audit outcome to the defined standard

Audit Report Preparation

- Present findings to Project Manager first
- Then, prepare final report

Audit Termination

- Review of audit process
- Disbanding of team

Responsibilities of the auditor

- As in medicine, "first do no harm"
- Be truthful, upfront with all parties
- Maintain objectivity and independence
- Acknowledge entering biases
- Project confidentiality
- Limit contacts to those approved by management

PHASES OF PROJECT AUDITING

Project auditing process consists of three phases:

Phase 1: Success Criteria and Questionnaire Development

- During this phase, the auditor interviews the core project sponsor as well as the project manager to determine whether their needs are being met.
- Open ended questionnaire is developed and administered on project team members.

Phase 2: In-depth Research

- Conducting individual research interviews with the Project Sponsor, Project Manager and Project Team members in order to identify the past, current and future issues, concerns, challenges and opportunities.
- Conducting individual research interviews with stakeholders including vendors, suppliers, contractors, other project internal and external resources and selected customers.
- Assessing the issues, challenges and concerns in more depth to get to the root causes of the problems.
- Reviewing historical and current documentation related to the project including;
  - Team Structure
  - Scope Statement
  - Business Requirements
  - Project Plan
  - Milestone Report
  - Meeting Minutes
  - Action Items
  - Risk Logs

- ○ Issue Logs
- ○ Change Logs
- Reviewing the Project Plan to determine how the Vendor Plan has been incorporated into the overall project plan.
- Interviewing selected Stakeholders to identify and determine what their expectations of the project had been and to identify to what extent their expectations have been met.
- Reviewing the Project Quality Management and the Product Quality Management to identify the issues, concerns and challenges in the overall management of the project and to identify the opportunities that can be realized through improvements to the attention of project and product quality.
- Identifying the Lessons Learned that can improve the performance of other future projects within the organization.

Phase 3: Report Development

Findings and recommendations are the core of an audit report. A finding is a conclusion related to an auditor's examination of problems and provides recommendations for corrective action in order to prevent their future recurrence. When the auditor has what he thinks is a finding, he will discuss it with the project manager. There are several reasons for this: the auditor wants to make sure the conclusions are accurate and document what the project manager's response is. In these conversations, the project manager should determine whether the auditor has the complete picture—and if not, be ready to provide evidence supporting his position. After all, the auditors are there for a short period of time, while the project manger has (ideally) been there since the project initiation, and from all perspectives, should understand the project best. There may be mitigating circumstances which the auditor needs to be made aware e.g. a variance not to follow certain procedures was requested by the project manager and approved by the management.

Findings are often categorized by risk: high, medium or low. If the project manager agrees with the audit findings but not the risk, he should discuss the reason with thee auditor.

During the audit, it is important the project manager keeps the sponsors apprised of any findings and any progress.

Lastly, the auditor finalizes the creation of the audit report and recommendations based on the findings and presenting this detailed report with the attendant recommendations including the Road Map to get future projects to the "next level" of performance.

THE IN-PROGRESS PROJECT AUDIT

How are you doing'?

Is this a silly phrase "How are you doing'?" In reality, no one really cares about how anyone is doing. But, in the world of projects, this is a critical concern. Yet, more often than not, we don't find out how we're doing until it is too late to do anything about items that are not going well.

Will we meet the schedule deadline? We may have some hand on that. How about costs? Are we within budget? Will we make the designed profit? Costs are a bit more difficult to track, but they can be monitored and evaluated if desired.

Will we deliver the intended scope? This usually gets less attention. Run out of time—we may remove some content. Run out of money—something has to go. Run into technical problems—a capability may be compromised or eliminated. The promised performance may not be delivered. But will we know this before we deliver the shortened project?

There are numerous ways to monitor project progress. We can monitor the critical path. We can monitor expenditures. Earned value analysis (EVA) is an exceptionally powerful and versatile capability and should be used wherever possible and practical. We should also be monitoring risk items and deliverables and, of course, quality.

However, this section is not about these important project management processes. Here, we focus on the client. Communicating with the customer and maintaining the client's satisfaction are paramount to a successful delivery.

What about Customer Satisfaction?

We think that we are pursuing quality when we survey our clients after we have completed the project. But what does this accomplish? If the customer is not happy, what options do we have to rectify this?

Certainly, the project post-mortem evaluation is important and valuable. This process would include evaluation of internal performance, as well as a survey of client satisfaction. We need and value this feedback.

The post-project review will help us to fix parts of our process that are deficient and (if we learned anything) to do a better job next time. But what about catching these problems during execution of the current job?

Early Detection

What if we could evaluate all of this while we are engaged in the project, rather than when we are through? What if we had a current evaluation of how we were doing with schedule, costs, scope, and, especially, customer satisfaction? This is the benefit of the In-Progress Project Audit.

What we are looking for here is to improve the eventual satisfaction of the customer/sponsor by taking the pulse of the project at one or more stages during its execution.

The In-Progress Project Audit (IPPA)

The primary mechanism of the IPPA is the **stakeholder survey**. A questionnaire is prepared to query the various key stakeholders about a wide-range of aspects of the job. Most of the measurements are qualitative, rather than quantitative.

What you are looking for is an evaluation of "How are we doing?" Through the IPPA survey, you are asking the stakeholders to evaluate your project team's performance on the subject project. The questions should elicit a frank response, even if that response might be critical of the project team.

Your primary objective is not to get a "high score" on the survey, but rather to gain high stakeholder satisfaction when the job is done.

Example of a Measurement Area

Below, is an example of one possible measurement area that could appear on the survey. The first column presents three questions, to be scored by the interviewee. The second column presents the range of conditions that would be used to score the questions. The poorest condition gets a score of "1". The best condition gets a score of "5".

Item Set: Resource Quality and Skill Set

Verify the team size and skill complement, workday constraints and individual availability.

Resource Quality/Skills	Condition	Score
1. Resources defined and assigned	1. Insufficient to meet project scope/needs	= 1
2. Resources trained in work scope and tools	2. Meeting needs, average quality	= 3

3. Resources available as needed	3. Exceeding expectations and work quality exceeding expectations	= 5

There is no limit to the range or number of questions. The survey should be designed to reflect the nature of the services provided and the areas that you desire to explore. There will be significant variations of the IPPA, reflecting the wide range of types of projects and services.

The survey is conducted across a broad range of client personnel. We are looking for at least one representative of each involved discipline. Where there is an individual score (issue) that is unsatisfactory, it might indicate a personal problem. However, when an issue garners a low score across a large portion of the survey group, we're no doubt looking at something that needs to be addressed.

Case Study

You may be surprised by what comes out in the survey. Jadala was involved in one IPPA where he was brought in as an independent third-party to survey a large organization that had engaged a consulting firm to develop a new HR policy document. In interviewing the client firm, one issue repeatedly came up. Several people felt uncomfortable with the person who was conducting training for this project. They complained that this person came on too strong and was intimidating. This created a difficult relations problem for Jadala, because the trainer at one time was Jadala's Lecturer. Nevertheless, the message was clear and the survey brought it out in the open, enabling the situation to be remedied.

Who Conducts the In-Progress Project Audit?

The IPPA is best performed by someone who is **not directly involved** in providing the project services. This can be someone in an adjunct role within the firm. Therefore, the IPPA should be performed by an independent third party.

The independent evaluator has no territory to protect and need not fear hurt feelings. The people being interviewed can be brutally frank. The evaluator can filter the findings, getting them to the right people, in a manner that can promote the desired response.

A good interviewer will go beyond the itemized questions on the survey. Areas of dissatisfaction will often be revealed during discussion. The interviewer should add a comment section to record this feedback.

Make the IPPA a Selling Point

Most customers are looking for quality. Most contractors are looking for a sales edge. Adding the IPPA to the offered scope of services shows that you care about customer satisfaction, and gives you an edge on the competition.

1. This is a strong win-win situation. With IPPA, you:
2. Improve customer and stakeholder satisfaction
3. Improve project performance (by catching problems earlier)
4. Detect and correct project team deficiencies
5. Show that you care about the client and about meeting your commitments
6. Improve overall communications

Project Quality Assurance

Quality assurance, project management, and risk management are mature concepts implemented in various technological sectors of industry and government. They are dynamic in definition, methodology, application, and outcome.

Quality Assurance

In general, **quality assurance** is a process which encompasses any activity that is concerned with assessing and improving the merit or the worth of a development intervention or its compliance with given standards (Kusek and Rist, 2004). Quality assurance enables the implementing agency satisfies its technical and administrative performance requirements relatively free from discrepancies while meeting the stakeholders' needs. Quality assurance must be a part of an organization's culture to ensure all of its products and services are of the highest quality. **Project management** is the process of planning, directing, and evaluating the development and implementation of a project. **Risk management** is an aspect of project management that entails identifying risks and developing ways to eliminate or mitigate those risks. Each of these functions must be present and actively supported in an organization to effectively direct a positive project outcome.

Quality management is not an event—it is a process, and a mindset. A faulty process cannot produce a consistently high quality product. There needs to be a repetitive cycle of measuring quality and updating processes. To make the quality management process work, collecting metrics is vital and those metrics need to be defined in the initial stages of the project.

Project quality is not the responsibility of one or two people. It is everyone's responsibility. All of the team, including the customer, has a stake in ensuring that the deliverables produced are of high quality.

Everyone is also responsible for surfacing ideas for improvement to the processes used to create the deliverables

Quality Assurance Team Objectives

The Quality Assurance Team establishes objectives to support its primary goal to increase the probability that project resources will be successful in creating the deliverables. Through project oversight activities such as quality assurance review, risk analysis, and project monitoring, the QAT strives to ensure successful outcomes.

> *A successful project is one that achieves the desired effect on the agency and project strategic outcome measures within the planned cost and schedule.*

The focus of Project Quality Assurance Review is on major project resources in order to maximize successful outcomes. To achieve this, the following strategies are employed by the QAT:

1. Identify and analyze the risks to successful project outcome.
2. Develop the appropriate management and project controls to minimize those risks.
3. Monitor the project to:
   a. ensure effective management and project controls are in place and utilized.
   b. provide information to develop models to support future project planning.

The QAT intends to coordinate oversight and monitoring functions with a view to ensure that best practices are employed to guide the planning and administration of projects.

The following list identifies the aspects the QAT would focus on:

1. Initial Project Risk Analysis
2. Project Development Plan
3. Risk Analysis
4. Risk Management
5. Project Monitoring
6. Post-Implementation Evaluation Review

Project Auditors believe that a project quality audit should achieve three goals:

- To identify existing problems on the project
- To identify areas where problems may occur if changes are not made
- To support the resolution of problems by recommending where changes should be made.

The initial quality assessment consists of examining the current business processes to understand what the system provides today. It is performed to establish a baseline for the improvement of current processes, i.e., what is in place and working effectively today, what processes need improvement, and/or what processes need to be added or deleted. The assessment will include but not be limited to the following processes:

- Defined Project Development Life Cycle
- Project Management
- Project Planning
- Estimation
- Budget Management
- Resource Management
- Schedule Management
- Risk Management

- Requirements Management
- Configuration/Change Management
- Sub-Contract Management
- Project Analysis & Design Approach
- Construction (Code) Approach
- Verification & Validation (Testing) Approach
- Defect Management

Within each category noted above, the processes are evaluated as to their completeness, utilizing the process workbench approach. Process components include:

- Policy
- Standards—Product Attributes
- Standards—Process Requirements
- Inputs required
- Tasks or Step-by-Step Procedures
- Quality Control Procedures
- Data Capture Methods for Measurements
- Tools Support
- Output Product

A single person rarely causes problems on projects. They are usually the result of either missing or inadequate processes or failure to follow the processes.

As projects and programs become increasingly complex, executive management may not have a clear understanding of the project's status or problems. They often wonder:

- What are the project's risks? How are these risks being managed and mitigated?
- Will the project meet its objectives?

- Is the project still aligned with our strategic goals—or has it gone off on a tangent?
- Are the project reports an accurate reflection of reality?
- What is the quality of the deliverables?
- Has the contractor fulfilled all of the contractual obligations?
- Are industry standards being used on the project?
- Is the contractor giving me inexperienced personnel, with my project doing the training?

These concerns are especially valid when contracts are structured so that the contractor's goals are not aligned with the client's, as may occur in fixed price contracts.

A project quality audit (sometimes called a Quality Assurance Review) and subsequent action plan will improve business processes within the organization. Ideally, a contract should include the option for such an independent assessment or some other means to assure that the project is on track and will deliver the quality the client expects to the schedule and budget that was promised.

A quality report is generated using a tested methodology and provides the following:

- An independent perspective, with unbiased insight on project status and results
- Assessment of the quality of project deliverables
- Evaluation against best practices
- Recommendations and alternatives.

Measures

Measures of the project progress, product quality, and process performance include the following:

Milestone Attainment—Monitor achievement of milestones to the initial milestones set in the project plan, reporting variance on each; maintain the initial baseline, as well as the most recent update; report achievement and variance to both

Effort Spent—Track the initial effort estimates for each major element of the work breakdown structure, compared to the actual effort spent performing that element (may be a work product or an activity)

Budget/Cost Performance—Track the rate of spending on the project by period (week or month) compared to the planned spending

Requirements Change—Track requirements change by period (generally month), showing total number of requirements, number added in this period, number deleted in this period, and number changed in this period; also track these dimensions by the amount of effort reflected in each, to understand the impact on the project's time and cost

Measures for monitoring the project monitoring and controlling activities include the following:

Handling of Project Tracking—Use items such as

- Schedule attainment—compare progress review dates to the dates planned
- Effort required—compare the amount of effort used for monitoring and controlling to the plan

VERIFICATION ACTIVITIES DURING PROJECT MONITORING AND CONTROL

During project monitoring and control, the following verification activities are appropriate for management:

- Review periodic reports of the project team and/or project manager, to ensure that the project continues to meet business needs.
- Provide information as needed by the project, and authorize the work to proceed if the project is meeting plans and commitments.
- Participate in formal project reviews, reviewing status and handling action items.
- Review the business case (or cost/benefit analysis, as appropriate) on a regular basis, to ensure that this project should continue.

The following verification activities are appropriate for Quality Assurance:

- Review activities of the project team on an ongoing basis, to verify that they are following their plan and the relevant processes of the organization.
- Review the results of work product reviews and testing, to ensure that the project deliverables meet customer requirements and project quality plans.
- Review change management and configuration management activities, to ensure they follow the organization processes and that baseline are under control.

QUALITY ASSURANCE AND PROJECT MONITORING

The Quality Assurance Team (QAT) monitors a project to ensure it has the means to meet its objectives. Project monitoring determines when a deviation from the plan occurs and assesses the impact of that deviation on overall project delivery.

Purpose of Project Monitoring

The monitoring process is intended to aid the Quality Assurance Team in identifying areas of high risk and possible failure points. After identification, appropriate corrective action should be taken to assure the success of the project. During the course of project monitoring and review, if a project is determined to be failing and unable to meet its objectives, the role of the QAT is to advise the leadership to discontinue the investment.

The purpose of project monitoring is to detect

- Processes or outputs that deviate from the plan(s)
- Risks that are identified in the risk analysis by project management
- Processes that do not effectively address quality assurance in performance or product delivery
- Areas where costs are not in accordance with the budget

Additionally, project monitoring will enable the QAT to identify:

- Best practices that can be shared with all agencies, and
- Successful projects that could be used as models for other agencies.

PROJECT MONITORING PROCESS DESCRIPTION

Project monitoring begins after the QAT determines the project meets the criteria for Quality Assurance Review. The level of monitoring is assigned by the QAT and typically corresponds to the project risk level assessment.

Monitoring can begin in the initial planning stages or commence later in the project and generally continues through the implementation phase. Post implementation monitoring consists of verifying that the agency evaluates the benefits and other performance measures realized against those predicted to determine if the project met its goals and objectives.

The QAT continually assesses project information to ensure that an appropriate level of monitoring, corresponding to the level of risk determined by the Team, is maintained. Review of project information can occur throughout all project phases. The QAT determines and adjusts its monitoring level based upon its review of the product submitted by the agency upon completion of each step.

A list of the steps, the products, and the corresponding QAT monitoring decision points is provided in the following table:

Step	Description	Product	QAT Review Decision
1	If a project meets the criteria for Quality Assurance Review, the QAT may request the agency to complete and submit to the QAT an . . .	Initial project risk analysis questionnaire	Upon its review, the QAT assigns an initial risk level and a corresponding monitoring level, and/or requests additional input.
2	Based on the initial risk level assigned by the QAT, it may request the agency to submit to the QAT a . . .	Project Development Plan	Upon its review, the QAT assigns an initial risk and monitoring level, or retains or adjusts those levels, and/or requests additional input.
3	Based on information provided in the PDP, the Q agency to conduct, produce, and submit to AT may request the QAT an . . .	. . . independent risk analysis and risk management plan	Upon its review of both documents, the QAT retains or adjusts its risk/ monitoring levels.

Agency P Decision

Project reviews provide the opportunity for the QAT to review all pertinent information, that is, results of the internal or independent risk analysis, monitoring status, and any other available information, to evaluate whether the project is meeting its objectives. Monitoring enables the agency and the QAT to assess progress and determine if, or when, the agency needs to conduct and prepare, or update, its risk analysis and management plan. This can occur when:

- New, significant risks are identified,
- Risks potentially impact the objectives of the project, or
- Risks contribute greatly to the systems operational and/or support costs.

Generally, project monitoring and review continue through each phase of the project development life-cycle. The agency and the QAT work together in this process to evaluate the quality of the project development.

TYPES OF PROJECT MONITORING ACTIVITIES

The following types of monitoring activities are typically employed by the Quality Assurance Team:

- Attending user conferences
- Attending project meetings
- Attending executive briefings on project status
- Interviewing the project manager, project team, users, and agency executive management
- Validating the project management processes, change control process, project tracking and status reporting mechanisms

- Comparing project status reports with the PDP to determine timeliness
- Visiting the project site to assess project progress
- Evaluating project expenditures, both staff time and other expenses, and comparing expenditures with projections
- Consulting with outside entities involved in the project development such as federal counterparts, other state agencies, user staff, consultants, etc.
- Meeting with Internal Audit staff to review the project plans
- Analyzing the Project Development Plan
- Evaluating agency quality controls for acceptance of project deliverables
- Analyzing the post-implementation evaluation review to determine the success of the project

As stated previously, the monitoring level generally corresponds to the level of risk identified. For the highest risk projects, monitoring could include most of the above activities. For other projects, monitoring might include QAT review of quarterly status reports, attending regularly scheduled briefings by project staff, and conducting random visits to the project site to assess progress as compared to project development plans. The level of monitoring will correspond to the circumstances of the project and the level of risk determined by the QAT.

ELEMENTS OF PROJECT MONITORING

Throughout the project development life-cycle, the QAT will review relevant project information as part of its monitoring process. Information that is reviewed and analyzed is, in part, provided by documents such as the Biennial Operating Plan, the initial project risk analysis questionnaire, the Project Development Plan, results of the internal risk analysis, and the risk management plan.

Patrick Gudda

POST-PROGRAMME OR POST-PROJECT MONITORING

When a programme or project has terminated, the Government should continue (in the case of national execution), or assume responsibility for, monitoring the sustainability of results regardless of whether or not an ex-post evaluation is planned.

The main objectives of post-programme or post-project monitoring are to:

- Assess the validity of the conclusions and recommendations of terminal reports;
- Determine the extent to which the recommendations of the reports have been implemented; and
- Assess the likelihood that the programme or project will produce and sustain a positive impact and identify any actions that may be necessary to help to ensure the sustainability of the results.

Post-programme or post-project monitoring can provide an additional basis for decision-making and learning, especially in certain cases. It is recommended for a cluster of programmes or projects with the same theme rather than for individual programmes or projects in order to test more systematically the validity and effectiveness of various approaches within a given context. It might also be particularly appropriate for sectors where a period of several years or even a generation is required to achieve the ultimate improvements in conditions and where such changes can be measured against widely accepted national indicators (e.g., the health and education sectors and interventions aimed at protecting or regenerating the environment).

Performance Checklist

Intended use of this checklist:

Used by a project team, quality assurance personnel, or project manager when reviewing measures of project performance.

ID	Response	Items to Consider
1		Do actual trends correspond to planned trends? If not, is the variance within tolerances?
2		Is the variance approximately the same each reporting period?
3		Are actual values within planned limits?
4		Is there no evidence of outlying values and other anomalies affecting the results?
5		Are sources of any outlying values and other anomalies understood and under control?
6		Do multiple indicators lead to similar conclusions?
7		Is all other project information consistent with these results?

CHAPTER TWO

EVALUATION

INTRODUCTION

In this chapter we define the concept of evaluation, what it is and why we evaluate, the role of evaluation in relation to monitoring and audit, and its role in the context of results-based management approaches (RBM). The content is based on a review of a wide range of evaluation literature from academia and international development agencies such as UNDP, UNICEF, WFP, OECD and bilateral donor agencies such as USAID.

PROGRAMME EVALUATION

A **programme** is a coordinated approach to exploring an organization's specific developmental / thematic area. A **project** is a particular investigative or developmental activity funded by that programme.

Programme evaluation determines the value of collection of projects. It looks across projects, examining the utility of the activities and strategies employed frequently, a full-blown programme evaluation may be deferred until the programme is well underway, but selected data on interim progress are collected on an annual basis. **Project evaluation**, in contrast, focuses on an individual project funded under the umbrella programme. Project evaluation might also include examination of specific critical components. The evaluation of a component frequently looks to see the extent to which its goals have been met (these goals are a sub-set of the overall project goals), and to clarify the extent to which the components, contribute to the success or failure of the overall project.

Evaluation may be of different kinds according to:

- Its timing prior to action (**ex ante**),
- During implementation (**in-vivo**),
- After completion (**ex post**).

Other classifications of Evaluation may be according to:

- Its **doer:** the ones involved in the performed action itself (**self** or **internal**) or an external body or consultant (**external**), or a combination of both.
- Its **focus:** either on **accountability** (summative) or on **learning** or improving performance (formative).
- Its **trigger:** evaluation is defined, carried out by entities and persons free of the control of those responsible for the design and the implementation of the action (**independent**), or by entities involved in its management or its steering (additional features):
- Its **driver:** this is led by donor or partner (**donor-led**, **partner led**), or by several authorities, and donors (**joint**) along with stakeholders (**participatory**).
- Its **reach:** this is when limited to one's performed activities (**self**).

Programme evaluation is a **management tool** used in the assessment, as systematic and objective as possible, of an ongoing or completed project, programme or policy, its design, implementation and results.

The aim is to determine the relevance and fulfillment of development objectives, efficiency, effectiveness, impact and sustainability. Evaluation is the process of analyzing the use of project resources prior to action (ex-ante) during (in-vivo) and after completion (post-mortem). Such an analysis is done for the purpose of making the necessary and relevant recommendations and suggestions aimed at improving project implementation and hence better use of project resources.

An evaluation studies the outcome of a project (changes in income, housing quality, benefits distribution, cost-effectiveness, etc.) with the aim of informing the design of future projects.

Bamberger and Hewitt (1986) describe evaluation as "mainly used to help in the selection and design of future projects. Evaluation studies can assess the extent to which the project produced the intended impacts (e.g. increases in income, better housing quality, etc.) and the distribution of the benefits between different groups, and can evaluate the cost-effectiveness of the project as compared with other options." Evaluation therefore systematically and objectively assesses the following aspects of an on-going or completed project:

(a) **Relevance**—whether the design of the project remains valid in terms of the problem(s) it addresses and its main design elements (objectives, inputs, activities and outputs)
(b) **Performance**—whether the project is being implemented as planned
(c) **Success**—whether the project has achieved its immediate and long-term development objectives and the desired sustainability of project results or impact (Singh and Nyandemo, 2004).

Evaluation Star
Emphasis may be put on each line between „extremes"

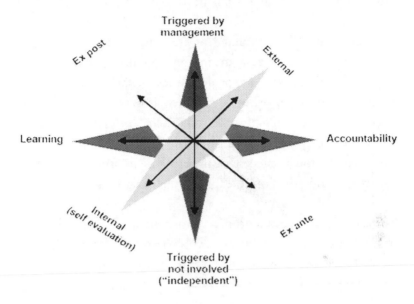

Evaluation is a periodic, in-depth analysis of programme performance. It relies on data generated through monitoring activities as well as information obtained from other sources (e.g., studies, research, in-depth interviews, focus group discussions, surveys etc.). Evaluations are often (but not always) conducted with the assistance of external evaluators.

Evaluation is undertaken selectively to answer specific questions to guide decision-makers and/or programme managers, and to provide information on whether underlying theories and assumptions used in programme development were valid, what worked and what did not work and why.

Unlike monitoring, which must be undertaken for all programmes and projects, evaluations are carried out more selectively for practical reasons. Programme or project managers have the flexibility to decide why and when an evaluation is needed based on a set of criteria.

If an evaluation is conducted at the mid-point of a programme or project, it may serve as a means of validating or filling in the gaps in the initial assessment of relevance, effectiveness and efficiency obtained from monitoring. It may also assess early signs of programme or project success or failure. If conducted after the termination of a programme or project, an evaluation determines the extent to which that intervention is successful in terms of its impact, sustainability of results and contribution to capacity development.

As in monitoring, evaluation activities must be planned at the country and programme or project levels. Baseline data and appropriate indicators of performance and results must be established.

EVALUATION OUTPUTS AND THE PROJECT/ PROGRAMME CYCLE

Stage of project cycle	Evaluation Output	Comments
Regular project supervision	Quarterly progress report	This will complement and be prepared at the same time as the quarterly supervision report sent to the funding institution. Whereas the supervision report is produced for use in validation, the progress report is designed for the project management and the project officer.
	Rapid feedback studies	More detailed analysis of issues identified in the quarterly progress report
	Intensive studies	Occasionally, these will be required to assist with project supervision
Mid-term project review	Mid-term project review	This will normally be a synthesis of existing studies even though additional data collection may be required
	Intensive or rapid feedback studies	This may be conducted to produce information required for the mid-term review

Project completion and audit	Final report	This will complement the project completion report submitted to the funding institution, or in some cases, the two reports may be merged
	Intensive or rapid feedback studies	This may be conducted to produce information required for the final report
Appraisal of second project	Mid-term project review or final report	Depending on the timing, one or both of these reports will provide inputs into the appraisal and design of new projects

Adapted from Monitoring and Evaluating Urban Development Programs, A Handbook for Program Managers and Researcher.

The table explains the various types of evaluation and when they are performed

Planning and Evaluation at the 3 levels of results:

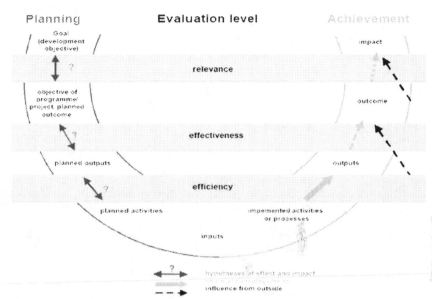

Look out: one may be very efficient but not effective! or very effective but not relevant!

To do things right is fine, but to do the right things is for sure far more important!

THE OBJECTIVES OF PROGRAMMES EVALUATION

The main objectives of programme evaluation are:

- To *inform decisions on operations, policy, or strategy* related to ongoing or future programme interventions;
- To *demonstrate accountability* to decision-makers (donors and programme countries).

- To facilitate improved decision-making and accountability this will in turn lead to better results and more efficient use of resources.

Other objectives of programme evaluation include to:

- Enable *corporate learning* and contribute to the body of knowledge on what works and what does not work and why;
- *Verify/improve* programme *quality* and *management*;
- *Identify successful strategies* for extension/expansion/replication;
- *Inform modification of unsuccessful strategies*;
- *Measure effects/benefits* of programme and project interventions;
- *Give stakeholders the opportunity to have a say* in programme output and quality;
- *Justify/validate* programmes to donors, partners and other constituencies.

EVALUATION STEPS

The evaluation process normally includes the following steps:

- **Defining standards** against which programmes are to be evaluated. In the logframe matrix, such standards are defined by the programme indicators;
- **Investigating the performance** of the selected activities/processes/products to be evaluated based on these standards. This is done by an analysis of selected qualitative or quantitative indicators and within the programme context;
- **Synthesizing the results** of this analysis;
- **Formulating recommendations** based on the analysis of findings;

- ***Feeding recommendations and lessons learned back*** into programme and other decision-making processes.

BROAD EVALUATION DESIGN STRATEGIES

According to Singh and Nyandiema (2004), the choice of an evaluation design depends on the

- Use that will be made of the evaluation results;
- Type of evaluation chosen;
- Resources available (time, money and skills available).

Kusek and Rist (2004) identified seven broad evaluation strategies used to generate evaluation information as depicted in the figure below:

Each is appropriate to specific kinds of evaluation questions. It is critical to note that only one of these seven is the classic after-the-fact evaluation i.e. the impact evaluation.)

Performance logic chain assessment		Pre-implementation assessment	
Process implementation Assessment	Rapid appraisal	Case study	
Impact evaluation		Meta-evaluation	

Patrick Gudda

PERFORMANCE LOGIC CHAIN ASSESSMENT

The performance logic chain assessment evaluation strategy is used to determine the strength and logic of the causal model behind the policy, program, or project. The causal model addresses the deployment and sequencing of the activities, resources, or policy initiatives that can be used to bring about a desired change in an existing condition. The evaluation would address the plausibility of achieving that desired change, based on similar prior efforts and on the research literature. The intention is to avoid failure from a weak design that would have little or no chance of success in achieving the intended outcomes.

In attempting to assess the present effort in comparison to past efforts, the evaluator could focus on the level of resources, timing, capacity of the individuals and organizations involved, level of expected outcomes, and so forth, to determine if the present strategy can be supported from prior experience. Likewise, in examining the research literature, the evaluator can find out if the underlying premises of the proposed initiative can be supported; for example, that increased awareness by citizens of government corruption through a public information campaign will lead to increased pressure from civil society for the government to combat and control the corruption.

PRE-IMPLEMENTATION ASSESSMENT

The pre-implementation assessment evaluation strategy addresses three standards that should be clearly articulated before managers move to the implementation phase. The standards are encompassed in the following questions:

o   Are the objectives well defined so that outcomes can be stated in measurable terms?
o   Is there a coherent and credible implementation plan that provides clear evidence of how implementation is to proceed

and how successful implementation can be distinguished from poor implementation?

o Is the rationale for the deployment of resources clear and commensurate with the requirements for achieving the stated outcomes?

The intention of such an evaluation approach is to ensure that failure is not programmed in from the beginning of implementation.

PROCESS IMPLEMENTATION EVALUATION

The focus of process implementation evaluation is on implementation details.

o What did or did not get implemented that was planned?
o What congruence was there between what was intended to be implemented and what actually happened?
o How appropriate and close to plan were the costs; the time requirements; the staff capacity and capability; the availability of required financial resources, facilities, and staff; and political support?
o What unanticipated (and thus unintended) outputs or outcomes emerged from the implementation phase?

The implementation phase can be short or long. The emphasis throughout would be to study the implementation process. Managers can use this information to determine whether they will need to make any mid-course corrections to drive toward their stated outcomes. This evaluation strategy is similar to monitoring. The added value is that the implementation is not just documented (monitored). In evaluating the implementation, unanticipated outcomes can be studied. Additionally, some of the more intangible aspects of implementation, such as political support, institutional readiness for change, and the trust in management to successfully lead a change effort, can be addressed. Finally, having some understanding of why the implementation effort is or is not on track gives a firm basis for initiating countermeasures, if needed.

RAPID APPRAISAL

Since M&E is viewed as a *continuous* management tool, rapid appraisals deserve special consideration here. Rapid appraisals can be invaluable to development practitioners in a results-based M&E system. They allow for quick, real-time assessment and reporting, providing decision makers with immediate feedback on the progress of a given project, program, or policy. Rapid appraisal can be characterized as a multi-method evaluation approach that uses a number of data collection methods. These methods tend to cluster in the middle of the continuum presented in the figure below

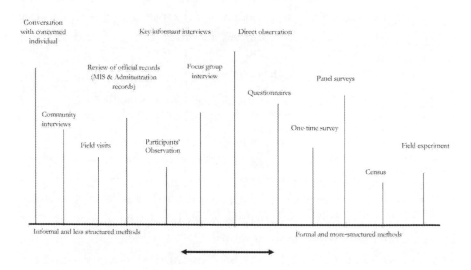

Adapted from Mercernt, 2000 cited in Kusek & Rist (2004) p.85

"Rapid appraisal methodology . . . [can be thought of] in the context of the goal of applied research; that is, to provide timely, relevant information to decision-makers on pressing issues they face in the project and program setting. The aim of applied research is . . . to facilitate a more rational decision-making process in real-life circumstances" (Kumar 1993, p. 9).

There are five major rapid appraisal data collection methods:

a) Key informant interviews;
b) Focus group interviews;
c) Community interviews;
d) Structured direct observation; and
e) Surveys.

These methods are particularly useful in dealing with the following situations:

o   When descriptive information is sufficient for decision-making
o   When an understanding is required of the motivations and attitudes that may affect people's behavior, in particular the behavior of target populations or stakeholders in an intervention
o   When available quantitative data must be interpreted
o   When the primary purpose of the study is to generate suggestions and recommendations
o   When the need is to develop questions, hypotheses, and propositions for more elaborate, comprehensive formal studies (Kumar 1993, pp. 21–22).

Rapid appraisals are highly relevant to the timely production of management—focused evaluation information. As with any evaluation method, there are some strengths and weaknesses of rapid appraisals that should be taken into account. Rapid appraisals produce needed information on a quick and timely basis and are relatively low cost, especially in comparison with more formal, structured evaluation methods. Such appraisals can provide a quick turnaround to see whether projects, programs, and policies are basically on track. However, the reliability, credibility, and validity of rapid appraisals may be more open to question because of such factors as individual bias and preconceptions, and lack of quantitative data that can be easily replicated and verified. Likewise, it is difficult to aggregate the findings from multiple rapid appraisals, as each is relatively unique and the mix of methods varies from one application to another. On balance, though, rapid appraisals can make rapid reporting possible and help flag the need for continuous corrections.

CASE STUDY

The case study is the appropriate evaluation strategy to use when a manager needs in-depth information to understand more clearly what happened with a policy, program, or project. Case studies imply a tradeoff between breadth and depth in favor of the latter. There are six broad ways that managers can draw on case study information to inform themselves:

- ° Case studies can illustrate a more general condition;
- ° They can be exploratory when little is known about an area or problem;
- ° They can focus on critical instances (high success or terrible failure of a program);
- ° They can examine selected instances of implementation in-depth;
- ° They can look at program effects that emerge from an initiative; and, finally,

o   They can provide for broader understanding of a condition when, over time, the results of multiple case studies are summarized and a cumulative understanding emerges.

IMPACT EVALUATION

An impact evaluation is the classic evaluation (though not only after the fact) that attempts to find out the changes that occurred, and to what they can be attributed. The evaluation tries to determine what portion of the documented impacts the intervention caused, and what might have come from other events or conditions. The aim is attribution of documented change. This type of evaluation is difficult, especially as it comes after the end of the intervention (so that if outcomes are to be evident, they will have had time to emerge). Obviously, the longer the time between the intervention and the attempt to attribute change, the more likely it is that other factors will interfere in either positive or negative ways to change the intended outcome, that the timeframe in which one was seeking to measure change is incorrect (too soon or too late), and that the outcome will become enveloped in other emerging conditions and be lost.

Another way of addressing the issue of attribution is to ask the counterfactual question, that is, *what would have happened if the intervention had not taken place?* Answering this question is difficult. But there are strategies for doing so, using both experimental and quasi-experimental designs. Use of random assignment and control or comparison groups are the basic means of addressing this question. When possible, it is best to plan for impact evaluations before the intervention even begins. Determining which units will receive the intervention and which will not, and establishing baseline information on all units, are just two of the reasons for planning the impact evaluation prospectively.

META-EVALUATION

Meta-evaluation is designed to aggregate findings from a series of evaluations. It can also be used to denote the evaluation of an evaluation to judge its quality and/or assess the performance of the evaluators. If a number of evaluations have been conducted on one or similar initiatives, a meta-evaluation establishes the criteria and procedures for systematically looking across those existing evaluations to summarize trends and to generate confidence (or caution) in the cross study findings. Meta-evaluation can be a reasonably quick way of learning "what do we know at present on this issue and what is the level of confidence with which we know it?"

CHARACTERISTICS OF QUALITY EVALUATIONS

There are six characteristics that can be considered. An assessment across these six characteristics will not guarantee that the information is impeccable or that it is error free, but it will provide a checklist for a manager to use in forming an opinion on whether to use the information.

(a) **Impartiality:** The evaluation information should be free of political or other bias and deliberate distortions. The information should be presented with a description of its strengths and weaknesses. All relevant information should be presented, not just that which reinforces the views of the manager.

(b) **Usefulness**: Evaluation information needs to be relevant, timely, and written in an understandable form. It also needs to address the questions asked, and be presented in a form desired and best understood by the manager.

(c) **Technical adequacy:** The information needs to meet relevant technical standards—appropriate design, correct sampling procedures, accurate wording of questionnaires and interview guides, appropriate statistical or content analysis, and adequate support for conclusions and recommendations, to name but a few.

(d) Stakeholder involvement: There should be adequate assurances that the relevant stakeholders have been consulted and involved in the evaluation effort. If the stakeholders are to trust the information, take ownership of the findings, and agree to incorporate what has been learned into ongoing and new policies, programs, and projects, they have to be included in the political process as active partners. Creating a façade of involvement, or denying involvement to stakeholders, are sure ways of generating hostility and resentment toward the evaluation—and even toward the manager who asked for the evaluation in the first place.

(e) Feedback and dissemination: Sharing information in an appropriate, targeted, and timely fashion is a frequent distinguishing characteristic of evaluation utilization. There will be communication breakdowns, a loss of trust, and either indifference or suspicion about the findings themselves if:

- ° Evaluation information is not appropriately shared and provided to those for whom it is relevant;
- ° The evaluator does not plan to systematically disseminate the information and instead presumes that the work is done when the report or information is provided; and
- ° No effort is made to target the information appropriately to the audiences for whom it is intended.

(f) Value for money: Spend what is needed to gain the information desired, but no more. Gathering expensive data that will not be used is not appropriate—nor is using expensive strategies for data collection when less expensive means are available. The cost of the evaluation needs to be proportional to the overall cost of the initiative.

TYPES OF EVALUATION

Evaluations may be categorized into two kinds or stages—formative evaluation and summative evaluation. The purpose of a formative evaluation is to assess initial and ongoing project activities. The purpose of a summative evaluation is to assess the quality and impact of a fully implemented project.

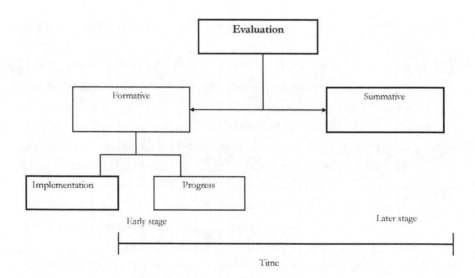

I. Formative Evaluation

Formative evaluation begins during project development and continues throughout the life of the project. Its intent is to assess ongoing project activities and provide information to monitor and improve the project. It is done at several points in the development life of a project. According to evaluation theorists Bob Stake,

> "When the cook tastes the soup, that's formative, when the guests taste the soup, that's summative."

Formative evaluation has two components: implementation evaluation and progress evaluation.

Implementation Evaluation: The purpose of implementation evaluation is to assess whether the project is being conducted as planned. This type of evaluation, sometimes called "process evaluation," may occur once or several times during the life of the programme. The underlying principle is that before you can evaluate the outcomes or the impact of a programme, you must make sure the programme and its components are really operating according to the proposed plan or description.

Sometimes, the terms "implementation evaluation" and "monitoring evaluation" are confused. They are not the same. An implementation evaluation is an early check by the project staff, or the evaluator, to see if all essential elements are in place and are operating. Monitoring is an external check. The monitor typically comes from the funding agency and is responsible for determining progress and compliance on a contract or grant for the project. Although the two differ, implementation evaluation, if effective, can facilitate project implementation and ensure that there are no unwelcome surprises during monitoring.

Progress Evaluation. The purpose of progress evaluation is to assess progress in meeting the goals of the programme and the project. It involves collecting information to learn whether or not the benchmarks were met and to point out unexpected developments. By measuring progress, programme staff can eliminate the risk of waiting until the prograamme has come to completion. If the data collected as part of the progress evaluation fail to show expected changes, the information can be used to fine tune the project. Data collected as part of the progress evaluation can also contribute to, or form the basis for, a summative evaluation conducted at some future date.

Progress evaluation is useful throughout the life of the project, but is most vital during the early stages when activities are piloted and their individual effectiveness or articulation with other project components is unknown.

II. Summative Evaluation

The purpose of summative evaluation is to assess a mature project's success in reaching its stated goals. Summative evaluation (sometimes referred to as impact or outcome evaluation) frequently addresses many of the same questions as a progress evaluation, but it takes place after the project has been established and the timeframe posited for change has occurred.

Summative evaluation collects information about outcomes and related processes, strategies, and activities that have led to them. The evaluation is an appraisal of worth, or merit. Usually, this type of evaluation is needed in decision making. The decision alternatives may include the continued funding, increased funding, continues on probationary status, modify and try again; and discontinue.

When conducting a summative evaluation, it is important to consider unanticipated outcomes. These are findings that emerge during data collection, or analysis that was never anticipated when three studies were first designed.

Evaluations may also be classified by agent, timing and scope.

I.   By Agent

- *Internal or self-evaluation:*—conducted by those directly involved in the formulation, implementation and management of the programme or project.

- *External or Independent Evaluation:*—conducted by those who are not directly involved in the formulation, implementation and/or management of the programme or project.

II.   By Timing

- *Mid-term Evaluation:*—Conducted at the mid-point of programme or project implementation.
- Focuses on: relevance, performance (effectiveness, efficiency and timeliness); issues requiring decisions and actions; initial lessons learned about programme or project design, implementation and management.
- *Terminal Evaluation:*—conducted at the end of programme or project implementation.
- Focuses on: relevance; performance (effectiveness, efficiency and timeliness); lessons learned about programme or project design, implementation and management; early signs of potential impact and sustainability of results, including the contribution to capacity development; recommendations for follow-up activities, including those being proposed e.g., second phase of a programme or project.
- *Ex-post Evaluation:*—conducted two years or more after the completion of the programme or project.
- Ex-post Evaluation is preferred for clusters of projects or programmes in a particular sector or geographical location or that concentrate on a specific theme in order to generate generic lessons and identify relevant policy issues. Ex-post evaluation judges the relevance, performance and success of the interventions at the programme or project, sectoral and thematic levels; Focuses on: relevance; performance (effectiveness, efficiency and timeliness); success (impact, sustainability and contribution to capacity development) ; lessons learned (best and worst practices, intended and unintended costs and benefits, applicability of lessons at sectoral and thematic levels

and across geographical boundaries) as the basis for policy formulation and future programming.

III.   By Scope

There are four types of evaluations based on:

- *Project Evaluation :*—Evaluation of a single project;

Focus depends on the timing of the evaluation.

- *Sectoral Evaluation*

Cluster evaluation of projects or programmes in a sector or subsector;

Focuses on: a comparison of the strengths and weaknesses of different approaches, modalities and/or strategies to address sectoral issues; collective effects of the programmes and projects on sectoral objectives at the country, regional and/or global level.

- *Thematic Evaluation*

Cluster evaluation of projects or programmes addressing a particular theme that may cut across sectors or geographical boundaries;

Same focus as that of a sectoral evaluation except that the evaluation is concerned with a theme that may also cut across sectors.

- *Programme Evaluation*

Evaluation of programmes (using the programme approach), and the portfolio of ctivities under the same management or fund.

Each of the types of evaluations categorized by scope may also focus on policies and processes. However, policy and process evaluations are described below as distinct types of evaluations to highlight their unique features. The strategic evaluation is included as a variation of the policy evaluation since it also deals with policies, but it is not concerned with policy impact. The timing of the strategic evaluation is crucial. Its main objective is to enable the various stakeholders to reach a common understanding of certain policy issues as a significant step towards policy formulation.

a) *Policy Evaluation* :—cluster evaluation of projects or programmes dealing with particular policy issues at the sectoral or thematic level

It aims to support policy-making by recommending new policies or changes in existing ones that are necessary to attain the sectoral or thematic objectives. The Focus is on relevance; implications or impact of policies on those directly and indirectly affected by them: costs and benefits; effectiveness of institutional arrangements to implement or enforce the policies.

b) *Strategic Evaluation:*—May be called for because of the following:

- Nature of the topic: cross-cutting issues with significant implications for the major development priorities of the Government and sponsoring agency and with high risks to stakeholders
- Urgency of a situation that needs to be addressed, which therefore makes the timing of the evaluation critical
- Widely conflicting views on the issues that need to be resolved.

It aims to: deepen the understanding of a particular issue ; reduce the range of uncertainties associated with the various options for addressing that issue help the parties concerned to reach acceptable working agreements as a step towards making timely decisions on the issues involved.

c). *Process Evaluation*

A cluster evaluation of projects or programmes to assess the efficiency and effectiveness of a particular process or modality they have adopted.

METHODS OF EVALUATION DATA COLLECTION

During the period of monitoring, one gathers information and data through the use of:

a) Questionnaires.
b) Meeting and interviewing people both individually or in groups, health workers, farmers, project personnel, local etc.
c) Documentary review—project profiles / business plan/ graphics.
d) Personal observations.

The right data and information is important for monitoring and evaluation effectively

Parameters to be evaluated

How do we ask relevant questions? Choose the relevant parameters, the criteria or index. These can be selected along the following lines:

- The breakdown of the development (set of interrelated projects).
- Break the development projects into project components such as building materials.

- Project components are then broken down into activities, which in turn are broken down into elements (resources) and functions.

ANALYSIS OF EVALUATION DATA AND INTERPRETATION

The tracking of an impact evaluation become meaningful to decision makers through the process of making sense out of it. This is achieved by analyzing the results and interpreting them

Data analysis

Data analysis is a process of bringing order to the data by organizing it into categories, patterns and trends. It takes time and requires good data management techniques, creating, intellectual, rigour / vigor, hard work and thoughtful work

Analyzing quantitative data

Evaluations can use many forms of qualitative entrepreneurship development programmes. Two of the most useful are:

a) Statistical analysis
b) Cost effectiveness analysis

Statistical Analysis

Statistical analysis occurs at four levels.

a) Descriptive analysis (central tendency)
b) Associational analysis (correlation, chi-square)
c) Inferential analysis

d) Causal analysis

Descriptive Analysis is the usual starting point for quantitative analysis. It focuses on measures of

i)   Central tendency-means, mode, median
ii) Measures of dispersion—standard deviation, variance, coefficient of variation.

Application:

In entrepreneurship development programme, it could focus on whether individual participated in the programme, have much training they received and how long ago was the programme.

Associational Analysis involves statistical estimation of the relationship between two or more variables. An association exists when the values of two or more characteristics vary in a systematic way e.g. positive or negative relationship.

Inferential Analysis refers to the use of data from a sample to estivate the values of the population from which the sample was selected e.g. association between individual sex and likelihood that he/she was selected to participate in the skills upgrading training programmes.

Causal Analysis is used to test whether a programme has actually had an effect. The capacity to reach a causal conclusion depends not only on a statistical association between the programme and outcome and impact variable, but on the analyst's ability to establish the proper temporal sequence and then eliminate the effects of other factors.

The analytical technique depends on the design used to collect data.

Example:

Did the participants who completed the programme perform their work more efficiently or effectively?

Cost-effective Analysis is used to assess the relative efficiency of different programmes designed to address the scored need. Conducting a cost efficiency analysis requires measuring costs and outcomes or benefits, wherever these can be clearly defined and easily measured. Final step in conducting a cost effectiveness study is to identify all the costs, even those not directly charged on the programme. Also identify individuals or organizations responsible for these costs. ll costs should be computed/quantified in accounting terms. Next compute a cost effectiveness ratio. e.g. cost per project team member trained divided by average value per unit of outcome such as improvement in the work programme.

Evaluations can also compute different programmes or different versions of the same programme to decide which one offers the best relative value, provided outcome measures across the programmes or versions are comparable.

Analyzing Qualitative Data

Quantitative data analysis can take many forms, the most common ones being :

   i)   Content Analysis
   ii) Case Analysis

Content Analysis

Content Analysis analyzes data drawn from interferes, observations and documents such as program description and memorandum reports. Once data is compiled, develop a classification system for the data. The classification should be organized in terms of:

- The evaluation questions for which the information was collected.
- The use to which the material will be put.
- The need for cross-referencing such as distinctions, between key variables such as country or institution will use important for analytical purposes and will need to be cross-referenced.

Case Analysis is designed for in-depth studies Evaluators may write a narrative data describing analyses of the case materials based on organized case record and by category. Several dimensions apply:—the

i) Analysis is relative, that is, data collection and analysis occur concurrently. Data is analyzed as it becomes available.

ii) Process follows the observe—think—test—review sequence. The evaluator makes observations then thinks about explanations for the data.

iii) Findings should be reproducible; meaning they can be tested with new cases or additional data.

iv) Analysis continues until evaluator's judge the explanation to be plausible and complete.

PLANNING AND MANAGING AN EVALUATION

Effective planning and management are crucial to the conduct of a successful evaluation. Several principles have proven to be particularly helpful in increasing effectiveness:

- Adequate preparations should be made prior to conducting the evaluation;
- Terms of reference (TOR) should be designed with the involvement of key stakeholders;
- A system to monitor the evaluation exercise substantively should be established.

Advance Preparation

Before the TOR is drafted, a few key questions should be asked and answered:

- Who initiated the evaluation?
- Why is the evaluation being undertaken?
- What products are expected from the evaluation exercise?
- Who are the stakeholders?

Formulating the TOR

Adequate time should be invested in formulating and refining the TOR. Key stakeholders must be involved in the process as much as possible so that their views and interests can be reflected in the TOR. To ensure the effective conduct of an appropriate evaluation, the TOR should contain the following elements.

(a) Introduction

The introduction should consist of a brief description of the programme or project and its objectives within the context of the development needs and priorities of the programme country and identification of the key stakeholders.

(b) Objectives of the Evaluation

In this section, the answers to the following questions must be clearly stated:

- Who initiated the evaluation?
- Why is the evaluation being undertaken?
- What will the evaluation try to accomplish?
- Who are the main stakeholders of the evaluation?
- What will be the scope of the evaluation?

(c) The evaluation sample

The evaluation sample should be described in terms of:

- The type(s) of programme(s) and/or project(s) that will be evaluated;
- Geographic coverage of the programme(s) and/or project(s); and
- Time frame of the programme(s) or project(s).

(d) Issues to Be Addressed by the Evaluation

The TOR should include a description of issues pertaining to the relevance, performance and success of the programme(s) and/or project(s) covered by the evaluation. The specific aspects of those dimensions will vary by type of evaluation. For example, issues relating to impact as a criterion of success are more appropriately addressed by an ex-post evaluation than a mid-term evaluation.

The TOR should also indicate that recommendations will be made and that lessons learned will be drawn from the programme or project experience.

(e) Products Expected from the Evaluation

This section should contain a description of the products that the evaluation manager wants to obtain from the evaluation, e.g., a particular strategy, recommendations on the best practices in a certain area or on the appropriate niche for sponsors interventions in a specific programme country.

(f) Methodology of Evaluation

The methodology that will be used by the evaluation team should be presented in detail. It may include information on:

- Documentation review (desk study);
- Interviews;
- Field visits;
- Questionnaires;
- Participatory techniques and other approaches for the gathering and analysis of data.

EVALUATION APPROACH

According to Singh and Nyademo (2004), we could employ the following approaches

a) **The experimental approach**

This is an orientation toward evaluation that seeks to apply the principles of experimental science to the domain of social programme evaluation. It aims to derive generalized conclusions about the impact of a particular programme by controlling extraneous factors and isolating programme influences. The strengths of the approach are its emphasis on objectivity and the generallizability of the conclusions reached using controlled experimental techniques.

The weaknesses of the approach include the difficulty of establishing controlled conditions in real world in which most social programmes operate, and its lack of sensitivity to the complexities of human interactions.

b) **The goal oriented approach**

One logical way to plan a programme is to identify a specific set of goals and objectives and organize programme activities to achieve them. The goal oriented approach uses programme-specific goals and objectives for determining the extent of success.

The strengths of the goal-oriented approach are its concerns with the clear delineation of logical relationships between objectives and activities and its emphasis on elements that are important to the programme.

c) Design focused approach

This approach emphasizes the systemamatic provision of information for programme management and operation. Information here is most valuable if it helps programme manger make better decisions. Therefore evaluation activities should be planned to coordinate with the decision needs of programme staff. The strengths of the decision-focused approach are its attention to specific needs to decision makers and the increased impact this may have on programme-related decision. The weakness of the approach stem from the fact that many important decisions are not made at a specific point in time, but occur through a gradual process of accretion.

Evaluation Team

The evaluation team should be specified in terms of:

- Number of evaluators and areas of expertise;
- Responsibilities and obligations of either party to the evaluation.

Implementation Arrangements

This section should consist of details about the following:

- Management arrangements, specifically the role of implementing agency offices (consultation with the offices and their prior approval when the evaluation is being initiated by headquarters);
- Realistic time frame for the evaluation process;
- Availability of documents for desk review;
- Briefings of evaluators prior to the commissioning of the evaluation exercise;
- Visits to the field, interviews, questionnaires;

- Debriefings; Preparation of report;
- Resources required being identified and made available;
- Arrangement of Logistical support needed.

While funding arrangements for the evaluation must be considered at the planning stage, they are not to be reflected in the TOR itself.

SUBSTANTIVE MONITORING OF THE EVALUATION EXERCISE

The staff designated for the evaluation exercise purpose must be thoroughly familiar with the TOR and work with members of the evaluation team to arrange effective monitoring of the evaluation exercise to ensure that the TOR are fully satisfied. Such arrangements may include:

- Briefings on the progress of the evaluation;
- Preparation of an issues report midway through the evaluation to indicate the preliminary findings of the evaluation;
- Validation of preliminary findings with stakeholders through circulation of initial reports for comments, meetings, and other types of feedback mechanisms;
- Formal debriefings with evaluators in the field and at headquarters.

Characteristics of Monitoring and Evaluation

Monitoring	Evaluation
Continuous	Periodic; at important milestones such as the mid-term of programme implementation at the end or a substantial period after programme conclusion
Keeps track; oversight analyses and documents progress	In-depth analysis; Compares planned with actual achievements
Focuses on inputs, activities, outputs, implementation processes, continued relevance, likely results at outcome level	Focuses on outputs in relation to inputs; results in relation to cost; processes used to achieve results; overall relevance; impact; and sustainability
Links activities and their resources to objectives by answering "what activities were implemented and results achieved?"	Assess specific causal contributions of activities by answering "why and how were results achieved?" Contributes to building theories and models for change
Alerts managers to problems and provides options for corrective actions	Provides managers with strategy and policy options

Self-assessment by programme managers, supervisors, community stakeholders, and donors	Internal and/or external analysis by programme managers, supervisors, community stakeholders, donors, and/ or external evaluators

Sources: UNICEF (1991). WFP (May 2004). ***Transformation of inputs into outputs through activities.***

RELATIONSHIP BETWEEN MONITORING AND EVALUATION

Monitoring and evaluation are intimately related. Both are necessary management tools to inform decision-making and demonstrate accountability. They are mutually supportive and equally important. Both use the same steps; however, they produce different kinds of information. Systematically generated monitoring data is essential for successful evaluations. Evaluation also supports monitoring. It can serve as a source of lessons that can be applied in the development of conceptual or methodological innovations for use in refining the monitoring function, e.g., devising appropriate indicators for future projects.

Monitoring and evaluation differ yet are closely related. Monitoring can provide quantitative and qualitative data using selected indicators, data that can serve as inputs to evaluation exercises. It may be argued that excellent monitoring precludes the need for evaluations. This is true only when the main objective is to obtain information on which to base improvements in a specific ongoing programme or project.

When a final judgment of the impact, sustainability of results and contribution to capacity development of an intervention is needed, an evaluation must be conducted because of the time factor: it takes a certain amount of time before sufficient evidence of results can be observed and attributed to that intervention. Moreover, when the objective is to draw generic lessons from the experience of a cluster of projects in a given sector or having a particular thematic focus, an evaluation is more appropriate because projects are monitored on an individual basis where as an evaluation can encompass one or many projects.

The relationship between monitoring and evaluation is best described as interactive. Neither function should be undertaken as a substitute for the other.

THE RELATIONSHIP BETWEEN EVALUATION AND AUDIT

Like evaluation, audit assesses the effectiveness, efficiency and economy of improvements, programme and financial management and recommends improvement. However, the objective and focus of audit differ from that of evaluation.

Unlike evaluation, audit does not establish the relevance or determine the likely impact or sustainability of programme results. Audit verifies compliance with established rules, regulations, procedures or mandates of the organization and assesses the adequacy of internal controls. It also assesses the accuracy and fairness of financial transactions and reports. Management audits assess the managerial aspects of a unit's operations. Notwithstanding this difference in focus, audit and evaluation are both instruments through which management can obtain a critical assessment of the operations of the organization as a basis for instituting

Difference between Evaluation and Audit

An audit is an examination or review that assesses and reports on the extent to which a condition, process or performance conforms to predetermined standards or criteria. It is concerned with resource allocation, financial and general administrative management and, to a certain extent, substantive issues.

Like evaluation, an audit requires the assessment of effectiveness and efficiency and the formulation of recommendations to promote improvement. In appraising these elements, however, audit differs from evaluation in orientation or objective (UNDP, September-1993).

EVALUATION, AUDIT AND RESEARCH

Learning + Accountability = Evaluation

Evaluation—Learning = Audit

Evaluation—Accountability = Research

An audit usually focuses primarily on compliance with existing rules and regulations rather than on establishing the relevance and determining the likely impact or sustainability of results of programmes or projects, which are the main concerns of evaluation. Notwithstanding this difference in focus, audit and evaluation are instruments through which management can obtain a critical assessment of the operation of the organization as a basis for instituting improvements.

WHEN DO WE NEED M & E RESULTS DURING THE PROGRAMME CYCLE?

During situation analysis and identification of overall programme focus, lessons learned from past programme implementation are studied and taken into account in the programme strategies;

- *During programme design,* data on indicators produced during the previous programme cycle serve as baseline data for the new programme cycle. Indicator data also enable programme designers to establish clear programme targets which can be monitored and evaluated;
- *During programme implementation,* monitoring and evaluation ensures continuous tracking of programme progress and adjustment of programme strategies to achieve better results;
- *At programme completion,* in-depth evaluation of programme effectiveness, impact and sustainability ensures that lessons on good strategies and practices are available for designing the next programme cycle.

Evaluation Report

The evaluation report requires pulling together the data collected, distilling the findings in light of the questions the evaluation was originally designed to address and disseminating the findings.

Characteristics of effective monitoring and evaluation reports

The reporting of monitoring findings/results is designed not only to convey information, but more importantly, to draw the needed reaction, decision, or action from the user/s concern. To achieve this objective, monitoring reports must have the following characteristics:

1. **Brevity**. The reports should be brief and to the point.
2. **Regular**. The reports should be prepared and sent out regularly to the user/s.
3. **Timely**. The reports should be timely and relevant if they are to be useful at all for decision-making or needed action.
4. **Specific**. Monitoring reports must be specific and situational and must be able to clearly state what the problem is and what action is needed and from whom.
5. **Uniform**. A monitoring report can be well compared with a road map so that the levels in a project organization should be able to find a standard.
6. **Flexible**. Not having a proper place for certain critical data or information should not deter one from including or highlighting in the same report. If an item clearly merits attention, it should be presented clearly and not "buried" in the mass of unrelated detail.
7. **Readable**. Clear labeling of sections, paragraphs, tables, charts, as well as clear, precise, and simple language should govern the presentation of the report.
8. **Reliable**. Verification and double checking of facts should be the minimum standard for the preparation of all monitoring reports. Any variance should be stated as such.

Sections of a formal report

- Formal reports typically include six major sections:
- Background
- Evaluation study questions
- Evaluation procedures
- Data analysis
- Findings
- Conclusions and recommendations

Background

The background section describes (1) the problem or needs addressed, (2) a literature review, if relevant, (3) the stakeholders and their information needs, (4) the participants (5) the project's objectives, (6) the activities and components, (7) location and planned longevity of the project, (8) the resources used to implement the project, and (9) the project's expected measurable outcomes.

Notable constraints that existed in when the evaluation was able to do are also pointed out in this section. For example, it may be important to point out that conclusions are limited by the fact that no appropriate comparison group was available or that only the short term effects of programme participation could be examined.

Evaluation Study Questions

The evaluation is based on the need for specific information, and stakeholders have somewhat different information needs. There are many questions to be asked about a project and they cannot be answered at one time. This section describes the questions that the study addressed. As relevant, it also points out some important questions that could not be addressed because of factors such as time, resources or inadequacy of available data gathering techniques.

Evaluation Procedures

This section of the report describes the groups that participated in the evaluation study. It describes the groups that participated in the evaluation study. It describes who these groups were and how the particular sample of respondents included in the study was selected from the total population available, if sampling was not used. Important points noted are how representative the sample was of the total population; whether the sample volunteered (self-selected) or was chosen using some sampling strategy by the evaluator; and whether or not any comparison or control groups were included. If comparison groups were included, it is important to provide data attesting to their equivalence or indicate how the problem of imperfect equivalence will be addressed.

This section also describes the types of data collected and the instruments used for the data collection activities. e.g.

- Data for identified critical indicators
- Ratings obtained in questionnaires and interviews designed for different stakeholders
- Descriptions of project activities from observations of key components of the project; and
- Examinations of extant data records e.g. letters, project plans, and budgets.

It is helpful at the end of this section to include a matrix or table that summarizes the evaluation questions, the variables, the data gathering approaches, the respondents, and the data collection schedules.

Data Analysis

This section describes the techniques used to analyze the data that were collected. It describes the various stages of data analyses that were implemented and the checks that were carried out to make sure that the data were free of as many confounding factors as possible. Frequently, this section contains a discussion of techniques used to make sure that the sample of participants that actually participated in the study was in fact, representative of the population from which it came. Any limitations in the generalizability of findings are noted. (That is, there are sometimes an important distinction between the characteristics of the sample that was selected for participation in the evaluation study and the characteristics of those who actually participated, returned questionnaires, attended focus groups, etc.). Again, a summary matrix is a very useful illustrative tool.

Findings

These are factual statements about the project/programme based on empirical evidence. The findings are usually organized in terms of the questions presented in the section on evaluation study questions. Each question is addressed regardless of whether or not a satisfactory answer can be provided. It is just as important to point out where the data are inconclusive as where the data provide a positive or negative answer Visuals such as tables and graphical displays are an appropriate complement to the narrative discussion.

Findings should enable a critical assessment of the project/programme in terms of:

- How the design of the project/programme ensured its relevance, efficiency, effectiveness, timeliness, impact, and sustainability of results
- The factors that affected project/programme implementation positively or negatively that those that are likely to affect its success or failure
- The results and implications to target groups and the larger environment.

At the end of the findings section, it is helpful to have a summary that presents the major conclusions. Here, "major" is defined in terms of both the priority of the question in the evaluation and the strength of the findings from the study. However, the summary of findings would always include a statement of what was learned with regard to outcome, regardless of whether the data were conclusive.

Conclusion

These are reasoned judgment based on a synthesis of empirical findings that correspond to specific circumstance. The conclusions section reports the findings with more broad-based and summative statements. These statements must relate to the findings of the project's evaluation questions and to the goals of the overall programme.

Recommendations

These are proposed actions to be undertaken under a specific circumstance, including parties responsible for that action. Recommendations must be:

- Clear and specific
- Related recommendations are clustered
- There are logical relationships among the findings, conclusions and recommendations
- Anticipated impact of each recommendation is stated.

Care must be taken to base any recommendations solely on robust findings that are data-based, and not on anecdotal evidence, no matter how appealing.

Lessons Learned

These may refer to lessons from experience that may be applicable to a generic situation rather than to a specific circumstance. It should include both the positive and negative lessons. The main factor to be considered in drawing lessons from experience is their applicability.

Other Sections

In addition to these major sections, formal reports also include one or more summary sections. These might be:

- An abstract: a summary of the study and its findings presented in approximately one-half page of text.
- An executive summary: a summary, which may be as long as 4 to 10 pages, that provides an overview of the evaluation, its findings, and implications. Sometimes the executive summary also serves as a non-technical digest of the evaluation report.

Utilization of Reports

The preparation of M & E reports is not an end in itself! Recommendations in the report must be carefully reviewed and acted upon, as deemed appropriate, in a timely manner.

Disseminating M & E results does not ensure implementation of recommendations and use of lessons learned. Active follow-up is necessary to implement recommendations made and to incorporate lessons learned in future decision-making processes. In some cases, project or programme management can easily take action on monitoring and evaluation recommendations. In other instances, it may be necessary for the main stakeholders to reach a consensus before action on the recommendations can be taken. Hence, it is good practice to organize a meeting with appropriate persons and institutions to establish implementation plan based on the recommendations and to identify specific responsibility areas.

FORMAL REPORT OUTLINE

I.   **Summary section**
    A.   **Abstract**
    B.   **Executive Summary**
II. **Background**
    A.   **Problem or need addressed**
    B.   **Literature review**
    C.   **Stakeholders and their information needs**
    D.   **Participants**
    E.   **Project's objectives**
    F.   **Activities and components**
    G.   **Location and planned longetivity of the project**
    H.   **Resources used to implement the project**
    I.   **Project's expected measurable outcomes**
    J.   **Constaint's**
III. **Evaluation study questions**
    A.   **Questions addressed by the study**
    B.   **Questions that could not be addressed by the study (when relevant)**
IV. **Evaluation procedures**
    A.   **Sample**

THE ROLE OF EVALUATION IN RESULTS-BASED MONITORING AND EVALUATION

International development organizations currently place strong emphasis on national capacity development, good governance and public sector transparency. In this context, evaluation, together with continuous monitoring of programme and project progress, is an important tool for result based management. In assessing what works, what does not work and why, evaluation provides information that strengthens organizational decision-making and promotes a culture of accountability among programme implementers. The lessons highlighted through evaluation enables institutions to improve programme and organizational performance. Demonstration of more and higher quality results through improved performance can lead to increased funding of assisted projects and programmes.

KEY FEATURES OF IMPLEMENTATION MONITORING VERSUS RESULTS MONITORING

Fukuda-Parr Lopes, and Malik (2002) identified the following key features

I. Elements of Implementation Monitoring (Traditionally used for projects)

- Description of the problem or situation before the intervention
- Benchmarks for activities and immediate outputs
- Data collection on inputs, activities, and immediate outputs
- Systematic reporting on provision of inputs
- Systematic reporting on production of outputs
- Directly linked to a discrete intervention (or series of interventions)

- Designed to provide information on administrative, implementation, and management issues as opposed to broader development effectiveness issues.

II. Elements of Results Monitoring (used for a range of interventions and strategies)

- Baseline data to describe the problem or situation before the intervention
- Indicators for outcomes
- Data collection on outputs and how and whether they contribute toward achievement of outcomes
- More focus on perceptions of change among stakeholders
- Systemic reporting with more qualitative and quantitative information on the progress toward outcomes
- Done in conjunction with strategic partners
- Captures information on success or failure of partnership strategy in achieving desired outcomes.

Many Applications for Results-based Monitoring and Evaluation (RBME)

There are many and growing applications for results-based M&E. As the needs for accountability and demonstrable results have grown, so have the uses and applications for results-based M&E systems.

PROJECT, PROGRAM, AND POLICY APPLICATIONS OF RBME

Results-based M&E systems have been successfully designed and used to monitor and evaluate at all levels—project, program, and policy. Information and data can be collected and analyzed at any and all levels to provide feedback at many points in time. In this way, the information can be used to better inform key decision makers, the general public, and other stakeholders.

Monitoring and evaluation can and should be evident throughout the life cycle of a project, program, or policy, as well as after completion. M&E—with its continuing streams of data and feedback—has added value at every stage from design through implementation and impact. "The specific information will also be different at each level, the complexity of collecting data will be different, the political sensitivity on collecting the data may change, and the uses of the information may change from one level to another" (Kusek and Rist 2001).

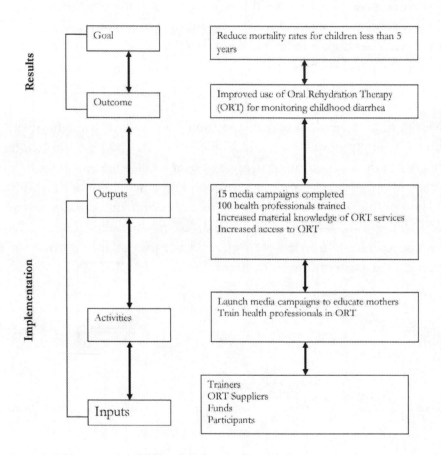

Illustrative Logical Model for a Health Sector Development Goal

Introducing the 10-Step Model for Building a Results-Based M&E System

Although experts vary on the specific sequence of steps in building a results-based M&E system, all agree on the overall intent. For example, different experts propose four—or seven-step models. Regardless of the number of steps, the essential actions involved in building an M&E system are to:

- Formulate outcomes and goals
- Select outcome indicators to monitor
- Gather baseline information on the current condition
- Set specific targets to reach and dates for reaching them
- Regularly collect data to assess whether the targets are being met
- Analyze and report the results.

Given the agreement on what a good system should contain, why are these systems not part of the normal business practices of government agencies, stakeholders, lenders, and borrowers? One evident reason is that those designing M&E systems often miss the complexities and subtleties of the country, government, or sector context. Moreover, the needs of end users are often only vaguely understood by those ready to start the M&E building process. Too little emphasis is placed on organizational, political, and cultural factors.

- o In this context, the 10-step model presented here **(Figure)** differs from others because it provides extensive details on how to build, maintain—and perhaps most importantly—sustain a results based M&E system. It also differs from other approaches in that it contains a unique readiness assessment. Such an assessment must be conducted *before* the actual establishment of a system. The readiness assessment is, in essence, the foundation of the M&E system. Just as a building must begin with a foundation, constructing an M&E system must begin with the foundation of a readiness assessment. Without an understanding of the foundation, moving forward may be fraught with difficulties and, ultimately, failure. It is Step 1. Throughout, the model highlights the political, participatory, and partnership processes involved in building and sustaining M&E systems, that is, the need for key internal and external stakeholders to be consulted and engaged in setting outcomes, indicators, targets, and so forth.

o **Step 2** of the model involves choosing outcomes to monitor and evaluate. Outcomes show the road ahead.

o **Step 3** involves setting key performance indicators to monitor progress with respect to inputs, activities, outputs, outcomes, and impacts. Indicators can provide continuous feedback and a wealth of performance information. There are various guidelines for choosing indicators that can aid in the process. Ultimately, constructing good indicators will be an iterative process.

o **Step 4** of the model relates to establishing performance baselines—qualitative or quantitative—that can be used at the beginning of the monitoring period. The performance baselines establish a starting point from which to later monitor and evaluate results.

o **Step 5** builds on the previous steps and involves the selection of results targets, that is, interim steps on the way to a longer-term outcome. Targets can be selected by examining baseline indicator levels and desired levels of improvement. Monitoring for results,

o **Step 6** of the model, includes both implementation and results monitoring. Monitoring for results entails collecting quality performance data, for which guidelines are given.

o **Step 7** deals with the uses, types, and timing of evaluation. Reporting findings,

- ○ **Step 8,** looks at ways of analyzing and reporting data to help decision makers make the necessary improvements in projects, policies, and programs.
- ○ **Step 9,** using findings, is also important in generating and sharing knowledge and learning within governments and organizations.
- ○ **Step 10** covers the challenges in sustaining results-based M&E systems including demand, clear roles and responsibilities, trustworthy and credible information, accountability, capacity, and appropriate incentives.

The 10-step system can be used for projects, programs, and policies. Though visually it appears as a linear process, in reality it is not. One will inevitably move back and forth along the steps, or work on several simultaneously. The use of such results-based M&E systems can help bring about major cultural changes in the ways programmes / projects operate. When built and sustained properly, such systems can lead to greater accountability and transparency, improved performance, and generation of knowledge.

SOME CHARACTERISTICS AND EXPECTED BENEFITS OF INTRODUCING RBME

The Expected Benefits of Strengthening Results-based Monitoring and Evaluation in Projects / Programmes

IF

- Senior management is strongly committed to the use of Monitoring and evaluation results in decision-making—commitment influences the management style;

- Staff undertake Monitoring and evaluation activities and use Monitoring and evaluation data at all stages of the programme cycle;
- Staff apply Monitoring and evaluation approaches to all areas of project operations for example in programme, finance, and human resources management;
- Staff engaged in monitoring and evaluation activities strive to pursue objectivity. They make clear the criteria and values on which their judgments are based;
- Staff are held accountable for results and take risks to achieve them;
- Staff apply lessons learned to programme management;
- Staff is recognized by the organization for achieving good results and for their efforts to counteract risks.

THEN

- The project becomes more efficient and better equipped to adapt to a rapidly changing external environment;
- The quality and effectiveness of project assistance increases;
- Project and its partners achieve results;
- Project's credibility improves;
- Funding for project assistance is likely to increase;
- Staff has a heightened sense of achievement and professional satisfaction; productivity improves.

Source: Adapted from UNICEF, 1998

PROJECT REVIEW

Review is a more substantial form of monitoring carried out less frequently (perhaps annually or at the end of a phase). This is usually done to assess effectiveness, relevance and immediate impact. It assesses whether the activities have delivered the outputs planned and the impact of those outputs. Key data sources for review will typically be both internal and external documents such as half-yearly or annual reports, a report from a stakeholder participatory review event, data collection documents, consultant's reports etc.

MONITORING AND EVALUATION AND THE PROGRAMME/PROJECT CYCLE

Monitoring and evaluation are integral parts of the programme/project management cycle. On the one hand, monitoring and evaluation are effective tools for enriching the quality of interventions through their role in decision-making and learning. On the other hand, the quality of project design (e.g., clarity of objectives, establishment of indicators) can affect the quality of monitoring and evaluation. Furthermore, the experience gained from implementation can contribute to the continuing refinement of monitoring and evaluation methodologies and instruments. To maximize the benefits of monitoring and evaluation, the recommendations and lessons learned from those functions must be incorporated into the various phases of the programme or project cycle.

1. Pre-Formulation: Searching for Lessons Learned

At the identification and conceptualization stages of a programme or project, the people responsible for its design must make a thorough search of lessons learned from previous or ongoing programmes and projects and from the field of development cooperation at large. A wide variety of sources of information are available from donor institutions, government offices and elsewhere. Those sources take the form of printed material, electronic media such as the Internet and computerized databases. Database facilitate the search for relevant lessons extracted from evaluation reports since the lessons can be sorted using multiple criteria (e.g., sector, country, region).

2. Formulation: Incorporating Lessons Learned and Preparing a Monitoring and Evaluation Plan

Relevant lessons learned from experience with other programmes and projects must be incorporated in the design of a new programme or project.

A monitoring and evaluation plan must also be prepared as an integral part of the programme or project design. Those responsible for programme or project design must:

- construct baseline data describing the problems to be addressed;
- clarify programme or project objectives;
- set specific programme or project targets in accordance with the objectives;
- establish consensus among stakeholders on the specific indicators to be used for monitoring and evaluation purposes;
- define the types and sources of data needed and the methods of data collection and analysis required based on the indicators;
- reach agreement on how the information generated will be used;
- specify the format, frequency and distribution of reports;
- establish the monitoring and evaluation schedule;
- assign responsibilities for monitoring and evaluation;
- provide an adequate budget for monitoring and evaluation.

A monitoring and evaluation plan is not intended to be rigid or fixed from the outset; rather, it should be subject to continuous review and adjustment as required owing to changes in the programme or project itself. The appraisal and approval of programmes and projects must ensure that appropriate lessons and a monitoring and evaluation plan are incorporated in the programme or project design.

3. Implementation: Monitoring and Evaluation as Support to Decision-Making and Learning

As noted earlier, since monitoring is an ongoing process, it can reveal early signs of problems in implementation. This information can serve as a basis for corrective actions to ensure the fulfillment of programme or project objectives. Areas of success can also be revealed through monitoring, enabling their reinforcement.

The contribution made by both monitoring and evaluation to lessons learned was also noted earlier. Thus, programme managers and other stakeholders must make certain that a learning culture is maintained throughout the implementation of a programme or project. Such a culture should motivate those involved in programme or project management to learn from their experience and apply those lessons to the improvement of the programme or project. Learning can be enhanced through participatory mechanisms that enable the various stakeholders to share their views and provide feedback when and where it is needed.

4. Programme or Project Completion: Dissemination of Lessons Learned

Upon termination of a programme or project, stakeholders as a group must take stock of the experience that has been gained: successes and failures, best and worst practices, future challenges and constraints. Special emphasis should be placed on identifying the lessons that have the potential for wider application, determining which particular user groups could benefit most from such lessons, and ascertaining the best way to disseminate the lessons to the target groups.

CONSTRAINTS AND CHALLENGES TO MONITORING AND EVALUATION

Certain conceptual and methodological constraints and challenges are associated with the monitoring and evaluation functions. Effective monitoring and evaluation can be achieved only through a careful, pragmatic approach to addressing these limitations.

1. Dependence on clarity of objectives and availability of indicators

Monitoring and evaluation are of little value if a programme or project does not have clearly defined objectives and appropriate indicators of relevance, performance and success. Any assessment of a programme or project, whether through monitoring or evaluation, must be made vis-à-vis the objectives, i.e., what the interventions aim to achieve. Indicators are the critical link between the objectives (which are stated as results to be achieved) and the types of data that need to be collected and analyzed through monitoring and evaluation. Hence, lack of clarity in stating the objectives and the absence of clear key indicators will limit the ability of monitoring and evaluation to provide critical assessments for decision-making, accountability and learning purposes.

2. Time constraints and the Quality of Monitoring and Evaluation

Accurate, adequate information must be generated within a limited time frame. This may not be a very difficult task in the case of monitoring actions since programme or project managers should be able to obtain or verify information as necessary. However, the challenge is greater for evaluation conducted by external consultants. The average duration of such assignments is three weeks; however, this should not be considered as the norm. The programme / project managers should have the flexibility to establish realistic timetables for monitoring and evaluation depending on the nature of the evaluations. Budgetary provisions must be made accordingly.

3. Objectivity and independence of evaluators and their findings

No evaluator can be entirely objective in his or her assessment. It is only natural that even external evaluators (i.e., those hired from outside the) could have their own biases or preconceptions. The composition of the evaluation team is therefore important in ensuring a balance in views. It is also crucial that evaluators make a distinction between facts and opinions. External evaluators must seek clarification with the other concerned parties on matters where there are seeming inconsistencies to ensure the accuracy of the information. This applies particularly to understanding the cultural context of the issues at hand. In cases where opinions diverge, the external evaluators must be willing to consider the views of others in arriving at their own assessments.

4. Learning or control?

Traditionally, monitoring and evaluation have been perceived as forms of control mainly because their objectives were not clearly articulated and understood. Thus, the learning aspect of monitoring and evaluation needs to be stressed along with the role that these functions play in decision-making and accountability. In the context of the project, the contribution of learning is to the building of community capacity to manage development should be emphasized.

5. Feedback from Monitoring and Evaluation

Monitoring and evaluation can provide a wealth of knowledge derived from experience with development cooperation in general and specific programmes and projects in particular. It is critical that relevant lessons be made available to the appropriate parties at the proper time. Without good feedback, monitoring and evaluation cannot serve their purposes. In particular, emphasis must be given to drawing lessons that have the potential for broader application, i.e., those that are useful not only to a particular programme or project but also to related interventions in a sector, thematic area or geographical location.

6. Responsibilities and Capacities

The implementing agency usually must respond to a variety of monitoring and evaluation requirements from donors. Within the context of national execution in particular, there should be only one monitoring and evaluation system, to eliminate duplication and reduce the burden on all parties concerned. Where the full capacity to carry out the responsibilities for monitoring and evaluation is adequately limited, the funding institution should assist the implementing agency to strengthen their monitoring and evaluation capacities or facilitate the engagement of external consultants.

CHAPTER THREE

PROJECT CONTROL

INTRODUCTION

Control is the act of comparing progress to set performance standards (plan) so that corrective action can be taken when a deviation, if any, from planned performance occurs. This definition implies the use of *information.*

Project control therefore involves compassion of performance against targets, a search for the causes of deviation and a commitment to check adverse variances. It serves these purposes:

- It ensures regular monitoring of performance.
- It motivates project personnel to strive for achieving project objectives

ACHIEVING TEAM MEMBER SELF-CONTROL

Ultimately, the only way to control a project is for every member of the project team to be in control of his or her own work. A project manager can achieve control at the *macro* level only if it is achieved at the *micro* level. However, this does not mean that you should practice micro-managing! It actually means that you should set up conditions under which every team member can achieve control of his or her own efforts. To do this requires five basic conditions. These are shown separately. According to Lewis (2001), to achieve self-control, team members need:

- A clear definition of what they are supposed to be doing, with the purpose stated.
- A personal plan for how to do the required work.
- Skills and resources adequate to the task.
- Feedback on progress that comes directly from the work itself.
- A clear definition of their authority to take corrective action when there is a deviation from plan (and it cannot be zero!).

The first requirement is that every team member be clear about what her objective is. Note the difference between tasks and objectives. State the objective and explain to the person (if necessary) what the *purpose* of the objective is. This allows the individual to pursue the objective in her own way.

The second requirement is for every team member to have a personal plan on how to do the required work. Remember, if you have no plan, you have no control. This must apply at the individual as well as at the overall project level.

The third requirement is that the person has the skills and resources needed for the job. The need for resources is obvious, but this condition suggests that the person may have to be given training if she is lacking necessary skills. Certainly, when no employee is available with the required skills, it may be necessary to have team members trained.

The fourth requirement is that the person receives feedback on performance that goes directly to her. If such feedback goes through some roundabout way, she cannot exercise self-control. To make this clear, if a team member is building a wall, she can measure the height of the wall, compare it to the planned performance, and know whether she is on track.

The fifth condition is that the individual must have a clear definition of her authority to take corrective action when there is a deviation from plan, and it must be greater than zero authority! If she has to ask the project manager what to do every time a deviation occurs, the project manager is still controlling. Furthermore, if many people have to seek approval for every minor action, this puts a real burden on the project manager.

PROJECT CONTROL SYSTEM

For effective project control, a system has to be put in place which specifies who reports what, to whom, and when. It is here the project manager makes use of various techniques like activity follow-up (to watch the general progress of various activities0, resources follow-up (completion of activities at the desired time) for reporting purposes (Singh and Nyandemo, 2004). The most basic model of a control system loop is shown in the figure below.

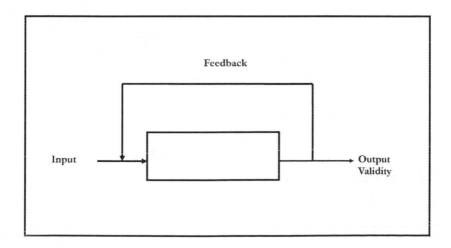

In this diagram, the output of a process is monitored by some means to determine the characteristics of the output. This data is interpreted and then feedback into the input of the process. On receipt of this information, adjustments are made to the process. By using this kind of 'feedback' control system, the performance of the process can be guided by the application of corrective actions to keep it within certain limits.

The monitoring point should be set so as to take a representative measure of the characteristics in which you are interested. The action that is taken based on the feedback is the corrective or control action which seeks to remedy the deviation that has been noted. The intension is to keep the system stable through regular corrective action.

CHARACTERISTICS OF A PROJECT CONTROL SYSTEM

The control system must focus on project objectives, with the aim of ensuring that the project mission is achieved. To do that, the control system should be designed with these questions in mind:

1. What is important to the organization? This will specify the performance measures to be selected.
2. What data should be used to estimate the current value of each performance measure?
3. What are the critical points in the process where raw data should be collected, from which sources and in what frequency so as to track and control the work?
4. How should the data be analyzed to detect current and future deviations?
5. How the results of the analysis should be reported, in what format, to whom and how often?

The answers to these questions underlie the design of the control system's data collection, data processing, information distribution, and response processes. Managers should exercise control throughout the project lifecycle. The information provided by the control system is essential for the on-going decision making aimed at keeping the project on track.

Several measurements can be taken in support of project control. These can be classified into four categories: schedule, cost, resources and performance. Project control should be exercised over what is important. On the other hand, what is controlled tends to become important. Thus, if budgets and schedules are emphasized to the exclusion of quality, only those will be controlled. The project may well come in on time and within budget, but at the expense of quality. Project managers must monitor performance carefully to ensure that quality does not suffer.

Taking Corrective Action

A control system should focus on response—if control data do not result in action, then the system is ineffective. That is, if a control system does not use deviation data to *initiate corrective action,* it is not really a control system but simply a monitoring system. If you are driving and realize that you have somehow gotten on the wrong road but do nothing to get back on the right road, you are not exercising control. Lewis (2004) cautions that, though, he once knew a manager whose response to a deviation were to go into the panic mode and begin micro-managing. He then got in the way of people trying to solve the problem and actually slowed them down. Had he left them alone, they would have solved their problem much faster.

Timeliness of Response

The response to control data must be timely. If action occurs too late, it will be ineffective. This is frequently a serious problem. Data on project status are sometimes delayed by four to six weeks, making them useless as a basis for taking corrective action. Ideally, information on project status should be available on a *real-time* basis. In most cases, that is not possible. For many projects, status reports that are prepared weekly are adequate. Ultimately, you want to find out how many hours people *actually* work on your project and compare that figure to what was *planned* for them. This means that you want accurate data. In some cases, people fill out weekly time reports without having written down their working times daily. That results in a bunch of fiction, since most of us cannot remember with any accuracy what we did a week ago.

As difficult as it may be to do, you need to get people to record their working times daily so that the data will mean something when you collect them. What's in it for them? Perhaps nothing. Perhaps future estimates will be better as a result of collecting accurate information on this project. In any case, you need accurate data, or you may as well not waste your time collecting them.

When information collection is delayed for too long, the manager may end up making things worse, instead of better. Lags in feedback systems are a favourite topic for systems theorists. The government's attempts to control recessions and inflation sometimes involve long delays, as a result of which the government ends up doing the exact opposite of what should have been done, thereby making the economic situation worse. There is one point about control that is important to note. If every member of the project team is practicing proper control methods, then reports that are prepared weekly are just checks and balances. This is the desired condition.

DESIGNING THE RIGHT SYSTEM

One system is not likely to be correct for all projects. It may need to be scaled down for small projects and beefed up for large ones. Generally, a control system adequate for a large project will overwhelm a small one with paperwork, while one that is good for small projects won't have enough "clout" for a big project.

Practicing the **KISS *Principle*** KISS stands for "Keep it simple, stupid!" The smallest control effort that achieves the desired result should be used. Any control data that are not essential should be eliminated. However, as was just mentioned, one common mistake is to try to control complex projects with systems that are *too simple!* To keep control simple, it is a good idea to check periodically that reports that are generated are actually being used for something by the people who receive them. We sometimes create reports because we believe the information in them should be useful to others, but if the recipients don't actually use it, we kid ourselves. To test this point, send a memo with each report telling people to let you know whether they want to receive future reports; if you do not hear from them, their names will be removed from the distribution. You may be surprised to find that *no one* uses some of your reports. Those reports should be dropped completely.

PROJECT REVIEW MEETINGS

There are two aspects to project control. One can be called maintenance and the other aims at improvement of performance. The maintenance review just tries to keep the project on track. The improvement review tries to help project teams improve performance. Three kinds of reviews are routinely conducted to achieve these purposes. They are:

- Status reviews
- Process or lessons-learned reviews

- Design reviews

Everyone should do status and process reviews. Design reviews, of course, are appropriate only if you are designing hardware, software, or some sort of campaign, such as marketing campaign.

A status review is aimed at maintenance. It asks where the project stands on the PCTS measures One of the common causes of project failures is that the project sponsor demands that the project manager finish the job by a certain time, within budget, and at a given magnitude or scope, while achieving specific performance levels. In other words, the sponsor dictates all four of the project constraints. This doesn't work.

The relationship between the PCTS constraints can be written as follows:

$$C = f(P, T, S)$$

In words, this says, "Cost is a function of Performance, Time, and Scope. Graphically, I like to show it as a triangle, in which P, C, and T are the sides and S is the area. This is shown in the triangles below.

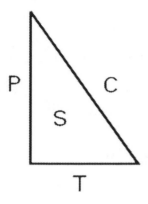
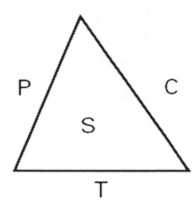

In geometry, we know that if we are given values for the sides of a triangle, we can compute the area. Or, if we know the area and the lengths of two sides, we can compute the length of the remaining side. This translates into a very practical rule of project management: The sponsor can assign values to any three variables, but the project manager must determine the remaining one. So let's assume that the sponsor requires certain performance, time, and scope from the project. It is the project manager's job to determine what it will cost to achieve those results.

Only if you know the value of all four of these can you be sure where you are. Process means the way something is done, and you can be sure that process always affects task performance. That is, *how* something is done affects the outcome. For that reason, process improvement is the work of every manager.

QUOTE

No problem is so big or so complicated that it can't be run away from.

—Charlie Brown(Charles Schultz, Peanuts)

THE THREE TYPES OF CONTROL

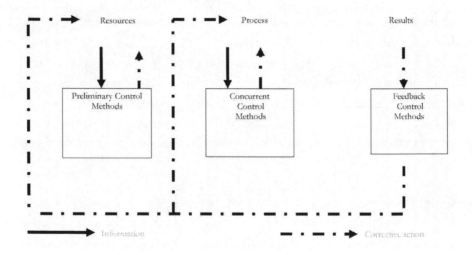

I. Preliminary control (feed forward control)

This is a control method focusing on preventing deviations in the quality and quantity of resources used in the project. Preliminary control is guided by the policies, procedures as well as the rules and regulations. Examples of preliminary control activities include:

a). ***Hunan resources*** must meet job requirements in terms of knowledge, skills and competencies mix. The team members must have the physical capacity to perform the tasks.

b). ***Materials*** must meet specifications and be available at the appropriate time and place.

c). ***Financial resources*** must be available at the right time and correct amounts.

d). ***Capital*** to pursue an adequate supply of plant and equipment

II. Concurrent control

Concurrent control monitors on-going operations to ensure that objectives are pursued. Concurrent control is implemented primarily by the supervisory activities of the project manager. Through personal, on-the-spot observations, the project manager determines whether the work of the project team members is proceeding in the manner defined by policies and procedures. Delegation of authority provides managers with the power to use finances and non-financial incentives to effect concurrent control.

III. Feedback control

Feedback control focuses on end results. Corrective action is directed at improving either the resources acquisition process or actual operations. Feedback control provides information concerning quality and or effectiveness of resources and processes. The results of Feedback control are used to guide future actions.

CONTROL OF MAJOR PROJECT CONSTRAINTS

There are three broad areas in which project control is critical. These are quality, cost and time. Controlling project work is mainly achieved by establishing work standards. Several techniques are used to control work, viz:

a). **Control point identification charts**

This chart sets out the critical control elements of a project. An example of this chart is set out below. It is possible to enlarge the number of control elements to include others such as people, benefits of the project etc.

Control elements	What is likely to go wrong	How and when will I know?	What will I do about it?
Quantity	Workmanship/ craftsmanship may be below desired levels	Upon personal inspection of each stage	Have standard work done
Cost	Cost of project subunit may exceed budget	When purchase agreements are made	First seek alternative suppliers then consider alternative materials

Time	Time to complete a project subunit may exceed schedule	By closely monitoring actual progress against schedule along critical path	Look for ways to improve efficiency Attempt to capture time from later steps Authorize overtime if budget permits

b). **Project Control Charts**

From project control charts, variance of each step are calculated and the cumulative variances i.e. the total, should give an indication of how well the project is being implemented with respect to cost and time element. When the cumulative variances appear to be large, it will call for the project manager to put in place mechanisms which can arrest any situation which appears to be getting out of hand. For the project control to be effectively used, it requires that measurements of performance be accurate as possible. The project manager should establish that the performance reflects the situation.

Cost (Kshs)	Schedule						
	Project steps	Budget	Variance		*Project steps*	Budget	*Variance*
Total							

Role of project manager in cost control

i) Setting up the cost control system in conjunction with the needs and recommendations of the financial function.

ii) Allocating responsibilities for administration and analysis of financial data.

iii) Ensuring costs are allocated properly (usually against projected costs).

iv) Ensuring costs are incurred in the genuine pursuit of project activities.

v) Ensuring contractors' payments are authorized.

vi) Checking that other projects are not using your budget.

c). **Milestone Chart**

A milestone chart presents a broad-brush picture of a project schedule and the control date. It lists those key events that are clearly verified by others or those which require approval before a project can proceed. In principle, a project should not have many milestones. Accordingly, most project managers find that milestones do not contain enough detail to help them control work. However, milestones provide a concise summary of the project progress. This is another way of monitoring progress that could be included in a progress report. The milestone slip chart compares planned and actual progress towards project milestone.

Planned progress is shown on the x-axis and actual progress on the y-axis. Where ctual progress is slower than planned progress, slippage has occurred.

A milestone slip chart is shown below.

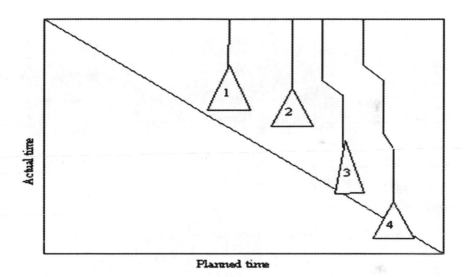

On the chart above, milestones are indicated by a triangle on the diagonal planned progress line. The vertical lines that meet milestone 1and 2 are straight—showing that milestones were achieved on time. At milestone 3 some slippage occurred. The chart shows that no further slippage is expected as the progress line for milestone 4 is the same distance to the right as occurred at milestone.

Ways of dealing with slippage. When a project has slopped behind schedule, there are ranges of options open to the project manager. These include:

Action	Comments
Do nothing	After considering all options it may be decided that things should be allowed to continue as they are
Add resources	If capable staffs are available and it is practical to add more people to certain tasks, it may be possible to recover some lost ground. Could some work be subcontracted?
Work smarter	Consider whether the methods currently being used are most suitable—for example could prototyping be used?
Re-plan	If the assumptions the original plan was based on have been proved invalid a more realistic plan should be devised.
Reschedule	A complete re-plan may not be necessary—it may be possible to recover some time by changing the phasing of certain deliverables
Introduce incentives	If the main problem is team performance, incentives such as bonus payments could be linked to work deadlines and quality
Change the specification	If the original objectives of the project are unrealistic given the time and money available, it may be necessary to negotiate a change in the specification.

d). Performance analysis

Variance analysis:—variance analysis involves comparing actual project results to planned or expected results. Cost and schedule variances are the most frequently analyzed, but variances from plan in the areas of scope, resource, quality, and risk are often of equal or greater importance. Variance analysis is inadequate in project control because:

- It is backward rather than forward looking. It tells only what happened in the past but does not answer the questions such as, what will happen in the future, is the work accelerating or decelerating?
- It does not use the data effectively to provide integrated control. The traditional variance analysis show whether in time period under analysis, more or less resources were expended than the budgeted. However, it does not indicate the value of work done. This information is valuable for purpose of project control.

Earned value analysis:—EVA in its various forms is the most commonly used method of performance measurement. It integrates scope, cost (or resource) and schedule measures to help the project management team assess project performance. EVA involves calculating three key areas for each activity.

i) *The planned value (PV),* previously called the budgeted cost of work schedule (BCWS), is that portion of the approved cost estimate planned to be spent on the activity during a given period.

ii) *The actual cost (AC),* previously called the actual cost of work performed (ACWP), is the total of costs incurred in accomplishing work on the activity during a given period. This actual cost must correspond to whatever that was budgeted for the PV and the EV (example: direct hours only, direct costs only or all costs including direct costs).

iii) The EV, previously called the budgeted cost of work performed (BCWP), is the value of the work actually completed.

These three values are used in combination to provide measures of whether or not work is being accomplished as planned. The most commonly used measures are:

- The cost of variance, CV = EV-AC
  NEGATIVE is over and POSITIVE is under budget.
- Schedule variance, SV = EV-PV
  NEGATIVE is behind schedule POSITIVE is ahead of schedule.

These two values, the CV and SV, can be converted to efficiency indicators to reflect the cost and schedule performance of any project.

The cost performance index (CPI = EV/ AC) is the most commonly used cost-efficiency indicator; (> 1, is over or < 1 is under budget).

The cumulative CPI (the sum of all individual EV budgets divided by the sum of all individual ACs) is widely used to forecast project cost at completion.

Also, the schedule performance index (SPI = EV / PV ahead > 1 or < 1 is behind schedule) is sometimes used in conjunction with the CPI to forecast the project completion estimates.

The project Time performance Index is computed using the formulae (TPI = ST / AT)

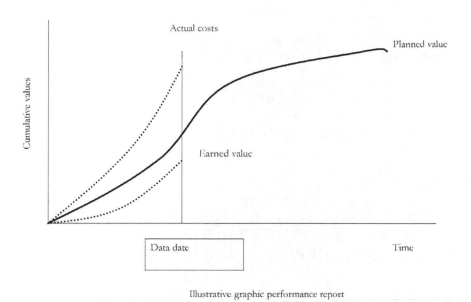

Illustrative graphic performance report

This S-curve displays cumulative EV analysis data.

EVM Worked Example

Problem: A project has a budget of KShs.10M and schedule for 10 months. It is assumed that the total budget will be spent equally each month until the 10th month is reached. After 2 months the project manager finds that only 5% of the work is finished and a total of KShs.1M spent.

Solution:

PV = KShs.2M

EV = KShs.10M * 0.05 = KShs.0.5M

AV = KShs.1M

$CV = EV-AC = 0.5-1 = —0.5M$

$CV\% = 100 * (CV/EV) = 100*(-0.5/0.5) = —100\%$ overrun

$SV = EV-PV = 0.5-2 = —1.5$ months

$SV\% = 100 * (SV/PV) = 100*(-1.5/2) = —75\%$ behind

$CPI = EV/AC = 0.5/1 = 0.5$

$SPI = EV/PV = 0.5/2 = 0.25$

$EAC = BAC/CPI = 10/0.5 = KShs.20M$

$ETC = (BAC-EV) / CPI = (10-0.5)/0.5 = KShs.19M$

Time to complete $= (10-0.5)/0.25 = 38$ Months

This project will take TOTAL KShs.20M (19+1) and 40 (38+2) Months to complete.

EVM Benefits

EVM contributes to:

- Preventing scope creep
- Improving communication and visibility with stakeholders
- Reducing risk
- Profitability analysis
- Project forecasting
- Better accountability
- Performance tracking

Illustrative tabular performance report

| | Planned | Earned | Cost | Cost Variance | | Schedule Variance | | Performance index | |
| | | | | | | | | | |
WBS Element	Budget	Value (EV)	Actual Cost (AC)	EV— AC	(CV/ AC)	EV- PV	SV- PV	WBS Element	Budget
Pre-pilot plan	68, 000	58,000	62,500	-4,500	-7.8	-5,000	-7.9	0.93	0.92
Checklists	64, 000	48,000	46, 800	1, 200	2.5	-16,000	-25.0	1.03	0.75
Curriculum	23, 000	20,000	23,500	-3,500	-17.5	-3,000	-13.0	0.85	0.87
Mid-term evaluation	60, 000	68,000	72,500	-4 500	-6.6	-2000	0.0	0.94	1.00
Implementation support	12. 000	10,000	10,000	0	0.0		-16.7	1.00	0.83
Manual of practice	7, 000	6, 200	6, 000	200	3.2	-800	-11.4	1.03	0.89
Roll-out plan	20, 000	13 500	18,000	-4600	-34.1	-6, 500	-32.5	0.75	0.68
TOTAL	257, 000	223, 700	234, 400	-16, 700	-7.0	-33, 300	-13.0	0.93	0.87

Performance reports organize and summarize the information gathered and present the results of any analysis. Reports should provide the kinds of information and the level of detail required by various stakeholders, as documented in the communication plan. Common formats for performance report include Gantt charts, S-curves, histograms and tables.

e). Budget control charts

These charts compare actual costs against budgeted costs. The chart gives a vivid impression of how well the budget is being controlled. The difference between budgeted and actual should be interpreted in light of time. When the differences are widening over time, investigations should begin.

PROGRESS TRACKING USING SPENDING CURVES: EXAMPLES

Consider the curves shown in Figure X and Y On a given date, the project is supposed to have involved Kshs.40, 000 (40K) in labor (BCWS). The actual cost of the work performed (ACWP) is 60K. These figures are usually obtained from Accounting and are derived from all the time cards that have reported labor applied to the project. Finally, the budgeted cost of work performed (BCWP) is 40K. Under these conditions, the project would be behind schedule and overspent.

Figure Y illustrates another scenario. The BCWP and the ACWP curves both fall at the same point, 60K. This means that the project is ahead of schedule but spending correctly for the amount of work done.

Fig. X : Plot showing project behind schedule and overspent

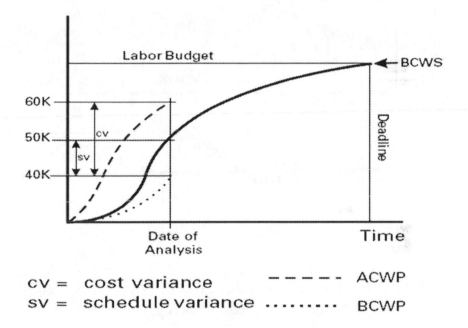

cv = cost variance   – – – – – ACWP
sv = schedule variance   .... BCWP

Fig. Y: Plot showing Project ahead of schedule, spending correctly

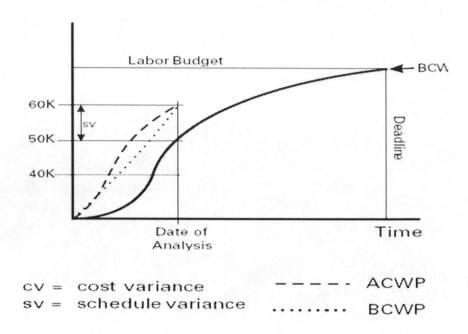

cv = cost variance   −−−−− ACWP
sv = schedule variance   ········· BCWP

The next set of curves illustrates another status. In Figure ZA, the BCWP and the ACWP curves are both at 40K. This means the project is behind schedule and under budget. However, because the manager spent 40K and got 40K of value for it, spending is correct for what has been done. There is a *schedule variance,* but not a spending variance. Figure ZB looks like Figure X, except that the ACWP and the BCWP curves have been reversed. Now the project is ahead of schedule and under spent.

Fig ZA: Project is behind schedule but spending correctly

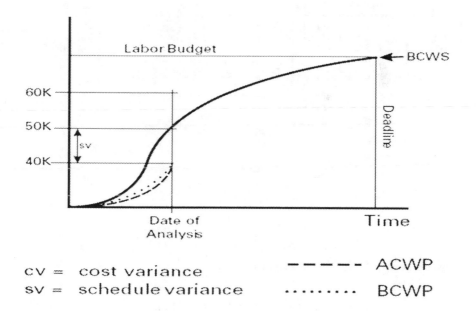

cv = cost variance

sv = schedule variance

— — — — — ACWP

· · · · · · · · · BCWP

Figure ZB: Project is ahead of schedule and under spent

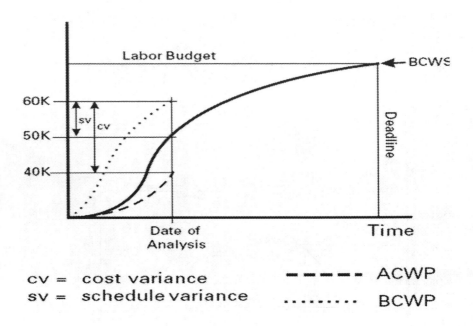

cv = cost variance   – – – – – ACWP
sv = schedule variance   ········· BCWP

Variance Analysis Using Hours Only

In some organizations, project managers are held accountable not for costs but only for the hours actually worked on the project and for the work actually accomplished. In this case, the same analysis can be conducted by stripping the dollars off the figures. This results in the following:

- BCWS becomes Total Planned (or Scheduled) Hours
- BCWP becomes Earned Hours (Scheduled hours   % work accomplished)
- ACWP becomes Actual Hours Worked

Using hours only, the formulas become:

Schedule Variance = BCWP-BCWS =

Earned Hours—Planned Hours

Labor Variance = BCWP-ACWP =

Earned Hours—Actual Hours Worked

Tracking hours-only does lead to one loss of sensitivity. ACWP is actually the composite of a labor rate variance times a labor-hours variance. When only labor-hours are tracked, you have no warning that labor rates might cause a project budget problem. Nevertheless, this method does simplify the analysis and presumably tracks the project manager only on what she can control.

RESPONDING TO VARIANCES

It is not enough to simply detect a variance. The next step is to understand what it means and what caused it. Then you have to decide what to do to correct for the deviation. According to Lewis (2001), there are four responses that can be taken when there is a deviation from plan. Which of these you choose will depend in part on what caused the deviation. Following are some general guidelines:

1. When ACWP and BCWP are almost equal and larger than BCWS (see Figure Y), it usually means that extra resources have been applied to the project, but at the labor rates originally anticipated. This can happen in several ways. Perhaps you planned for weather delays, but the weather has been good and you have gotten more work done during the analysis period than intended, but at the correct cost. Thus, you are ahead of schedule but spending correctly.
2. When ACWP and BCWP are nearly equal and below BCWS (see Figure ZA), it usually means the opposite of the previous situation; that is, you have not applied enough resources.
3. Perhaps they were stolen from you, perhaps it has rained more than you expected, or perhaps everyone has decided to take a vacation at once. The problem with being in this position is that it usually results in an over spend when you try to catch up.
4. When ACWP is below BCWS and BCWP is above BCWS (see Figure ZB), you are ahead of schedule and under spent. This generally happens because the original estimate was too conservative (probably padded for safety). Another possibility is that you had a lucky break. You thought the work would be harder than it was, so you were able to get ahead. Sometimes it happens because people were much more efficient than expected. The problem with this variance is that it ties up resources that could be used on other projects. The economists call this an *opportunity cost*. There is also a good chance that if you were

consistently padding estimates and were bidding against other companies on projects, you probably lost some bids. If your competitor is using average values for time estimates while you are padding yours, then your figures are likely to be higher, and you will lose the bid.

USING PERCENTAGE COMPLETE TO MEASURE PROGRESS

The most common way to measure progress is to simply estimate percentage complete. This is the BCWP measure, but BCWP is expressed as a dollar value, whereas percentage omplete does not make that conversion. When percentage complete measures are plotted over time, you tend to get a curve like the one shown in Figure ZC. It rises more or less linearly up to about 80 or 90 percent, and then turns horizontal (meaning no further progress is being made). It stays there for a while; then, all of a sudden, the work is completed. The reason is that problems are often encountered near the end of the task, and a lot of effort goes into trying to solve them. During that time, no progress is made.

Another part of the problem is in knowing where you are to begin with. We have already said that you are generally estimating progress. Consider a task that has ten-week duration. If you ask the person doing that task where he is at the end of the first week, he is likely to tell you, "10 percent"; at the end of week two, "20 percent"; and so on. What he is doing is making a reverse inference. It goes like this. "It is the end of the first week on a ten-week task, so I must be 10 percent complete." The truth is, he really doesn't know where he is. Naturally, under such conditions, control is very loose. Still, this is the only way progress can be measured in many cases.

Figure ZC: Percent complete curve

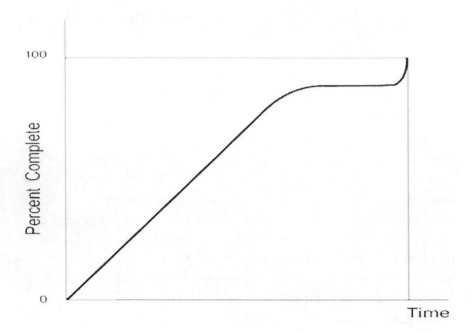

Reasons for Ineffective Control

a). Characteristics of projects.

Most of the projects are large, complex undertakings involving many organizations and people. This renders the task of control difficult because:

- keeping track of physical performance and expenditure on hundreds or thousands of activities, which are non-routine is a stupendous task.
- coordination and communication problems multiply when several organizations are involved in the project.

b). **People problems.**

To control a non-routine project, a manager requires an ability to monitor a wide range of disparate factor, sensitivity to symptoms indicative of potential problems and a faculty for comprehending the combined effect of multiple forces. Naturally, most of the operational managers, used to the steady rhythm of normal operations and routine work lack the experience, training, competence and inclination to control projects.

c). Poor control and information system.

One of the factors, which inhibit effective control, is the poor quality of control and information system. Some of the weaknesses observed in the control and information system are:

- *Delay in reporting performance:* This prevents effective monitoring of the project and initiation of timely action to check adverse developments
- *Inappropriate level of details:* Generally cost information for contract is collected in terms of cost codes found in the firm's cost accounting system, irrespective of the least of details employed for project planning and budgeting. Consider an extreme example wherein cost and value of work done are reported for the project as a whole. The big question is: what is the value of such information for identifying where slippages are occurring and who are responsible for them?
- *Unsuitable information:* One of the major problems in project control is unreliable and inaccurate data and information. Often project managers receive reports, which suggest that "everything is okay" or are "reasonably within control" when the reality is otherwise. Further, for months after the project is completed, costs dribble in to change a favorable variance into unfavorable variance.

SCOPE AND CHANGE CONTROL

Project scope is everything about a project—work content as well as expected outcomes (Pinto, 2007). Project scope consists of naming all activities to be performed, the resources consumed, and the end products that result, including quality standards. Scope includes a project's goals, constraints and limitations. **Scope management** is the function of controlling a project in terms of its goals and objectives through the processes of conceptual development, full definition, execution, and termination. It provides the foundation upon which all project work is based, and is therefore, the culmination of predevelopment planning. The process of scope management consists of several distinct activities, all based on creating a systematic set of plans for the upcoming project.

A **scope change** is any modification to the agreed upon project scope as defined by the approved WBS. Scope changes often require adjustments to cost, time, quality, or other project objectives. Scope change control is concerned with:

a) Influencing the factors that create scope changes to ensure that changes are agreed upon
b) Determining that a scope change has occurred
c) Managing the actual changes when and if they occur.

Scope change must be integrated with the other control processes i.e schedule control, cost control, quality control and others. According to PMBOK (2000) original defined project, technical baseline) must be maintained by continuously managing changes and incorporating them into a revised project baseline. Integrated change requires:

a) Maintaining the integrity of the performance measurements baseline.

b) Ensuring that changes to the product scope are reflected in the definition of the project scope.

c) Coordinating changes across knowledge areas e.g. a proposed schedule change will often affect cost, risk, quality, contract administration and staffing.

In the project context, the term scope may refer to:

- Product scope—the features and functions that characterize a product or service.
- Project scope—the work that must be done to deliver a product with the specified features and functions.

Completion of the project scope is measured against the project plan, but completion of a product scope is measured against the product requirements. Both types of scope management must be well integrated to ensure that the work of the project will result in delivery of the specified product. Controlling and managing scope change is critical to the success of any project, as scope changes can significantly impact the **cost, schedule, risks** and **quality** of the entire effort.

While scope is defined early in the planning and estimation phases, there are many reasons for changing it later on—for instance, a stakeholder may acquire additional insight into a problem during the course of the project. In addition to internal factors, external market conditions and government regulations often drive requests that extend beyond the initial project scope.

The key to successful scope management is defining, communicating and reconciling emerging requests throughout the project lifecycle. Change request comprise:

- Description of change required.

- Reasons for the change.
- Its priority, which may be mandatory, essential or desirable.
- The benefits of the change.
- Authorization of the project owner to raise the change request.

Why, What, How?

Definitions and Semantics—changing what?

The word "change" leads to many misunderstandings. It is used in different contexts depending upon what is being changed. In Project Management, there tend to be differing understandings of expressions like "Change Management" and "Change Control". The problems are compounded where participants are unfamiliar with project work and do not recognize the implicit context.

Here are some of the more common usages:

Scope Change	Where a request is considered to change the agreed scope and objectives of the project to accommodate a need not originally defined to be part of the project.
Change Control (sometimes referred to as "Change Management")	The management process for requesting reviewing, approving, carrying out and controlling changes to the project's deliverables. Change Control is usually applied once the first version of a deliverable has been completed and agreed.

Configuration Management or Version Control (sometimes also called "Change Control")	Technical and administrative control of the multiple versions or editions of a specific deliverable, particularly where the component has been changed after it was initially completed. Most typically this applies to objects, modules, data definitions and documentation.
Change Management	Normally used to mean the achievement of change in human behaviour as part of an overall business solution.
Change Programme	Usually used to mean a large, multi-faceted business solution (not just the human behavioral element).

In project management, remember that other people may be using them differently and that your team participants may be unfamiliar with the meanings. Try to make the context clear when you speak of "change."

Change is inevitable. During a project there will be many good reasons why things need to change. There will also be a few bad reasons—bad, but unavoidable.

Let's consider some of those reasons . . .

Change Driver	Comment
The business needs have changed	Business needs are changing ever more rapidly, particularly as competitors explore the new business models of eCommerce. All businesses must be willing to change if they are to remain competitive.
The organization has changed	It is surprisingly common to find that the organization undergoes some form of restructuring during the life of a project. This could involve mergers, acquisitions, being taken over, new departments, new business leaders, new products, new accounting structures, new locations etc.
Exploit technology improvements	The available technology improves constantly. A value-adding change such as an environmental remediation project is able to reduce costs by taking advantage of technology that was not available when the scope was originally defined.
The organization's priorities have changed	Although the scope and objectives of your project remain valid, the organization may decide that there are other business needs that have high priority and should be addressed.
New business partners and channels	Organizations are responding to the rapidly changing market place by forming new business partnerships and alliances. New business channels are becoming available through those relationships, e.g. using industry hub portals and intermediaries.

New legislation and regulations	There may be unavoidable external requirements over which you have no control, such as new regulations for data privacy, changed regulatory reporting requirements etc.
Globalization, standards etc	The organization is making progress in presenting and managing itself as a global entity and, hence, there are new or revised standards for such things as website design, database definitions, corporate knowledge sharing, data warehouses etc.
Effect of other projects and initiatives	Other initiatives within the organization result in revised needs for this project, e.g. there is a new accounting system so the interface from our new system will have to be changed.
An error or omission—we messed up	Or, to put it more discreetly, elements of the project's design and deliverables do not fully meet the defined need and will need to be re-worked.

SCOPE CHANGE CONTROL

Why is there a distinction between scope change and other changes? In general, Project Managers should pay a great deal of attention to managing scope. Allowing the project's scope to change mid-course usually means added costs, greater risks and longer duration. Many projects fail due to poor scope management. Very often it is a large number of small scope changes that do the damage, rather than the big, obvious ones. The successful Project Manager has learned that rigorous scope control is essential to deliver projects on time and on budget.

The world-class Project Manager would not express this imperative in the same terms. The prime focus for the Project Manager should not be to deliver the agreed scope on time and on budget, but to optimize the benefit that is generated by the project. If that means allowing the scope to change then that scope change is a good thing, not a bad thing. It is wrong to resist all scope change. Where a scope change generates improved benefit, it should be proposed to the project's decision-making body. Make clear the positive and negative impacts of allowing the change. Make sure the impact is fully reflected in the project's definition and performance criteria.

Watch out for the use of "scope change" as a defensive behaviour. In many cases, people will discuss scope changes in the context that a scope change is not the project's fault and must therefore be the business's fault. This is particularly important if the work is being performed by a different organization under contract.

Watch out for the use of "scope change" as an aggressive behaviour. Sub-contractors may intentionally try to expand the size of their contract by establishing scope changes that lead them to do additional work outside the original agreement. Some contractors under-bid the cost of the work to gain the contract, in the belief that they will be able to make their profit out of scope changes.

Classification of Project Changes

1. **Permanent changes** are carried out with the intention of leaving them permanently embedded in the design and execution of a project. They remain recorded as specifications to show true completion of a project.
2. **Temporary changes** that may be needed for expediting a project to completion. They are carried out with either the intent of removing them or converting them to some alternative permanent change at a more convenient time later.
3. **Change within the organization**

4. **Changes that originate from outside the organization**. This normally comes from change requests i.e. a request that any stakeholder can make. Change request must be in written form for documentary evidence.

CHANGE CONTROL VS. ISSUE MANAGEMENT

There are many similarities and much overlap between Issue Management and Change Control. A large percentage of "issues" will directly or indirectly being asking for something to change. Conversely, most changes reflect and generate issues.

Some Project Management approaches combine these into a single process, which can scare people away from communicating issues. Some others treat them as separate processes, which can cause practical difficulties, inefficiency and misunderstandings. Clearly there needs to be some linkage. The best scenario is to present Issues Management as separate but related processes whereby an issue can evolve into a change request where appropriate.

Basis of decision

The decision whether to accept or reject a change would be based on a number of rules. The fundamental logic should be:

Is the change unavoidable (eg legislative changes, mergers, etc)?

or

Does the change increase the overall benefit to the organization (taking into account any impact on the costs, benefits, timescales and risks)?

and

Is the Project Team able to make such a change?

and

Is the change best done now, or would it be more beneficial to defer it until the current work is complete?

SCOPE MANAGEMENT AT PROJECT START

Scope should be clearly defined as part of the Project Definition. Much of the work at that time is directed at agreeing the optimum definition of the project—both in terms of its deliverables and in terms of how it will operate. This scope definition will form the baseline against which potential changes are assessed and against which the project's performance is measured.

In defining how the project will operate, the Project Manager should try to influence those factors that could lead to subsequent scope change. The importance of a sound Project Definition should be emphasized.

Make clear the dangers and potential costs of subsequent changes of direction, but, equally, encourage the leadership to allow change where that would be beneficial. In the dynamic world of e-Business, rapid change is the norm.

All participants should understand that the later in the project that a change is addressed, the greater the likely impact in terms of ***costs, risks,*** and ***timescale***. It is wise to surface potential changes as early as possible. The change control process should make it easy to do so.

IMPORTANCE OF PROJECT SCOPE CHANGE MANAGEMENT

No one questions the relevance of change management for project scope, which can involve project deliverables, services, and work content. In particular, there are four strong reasons why scope management must be a top priority for the successful project manager:

1. **Cost:** Scope change can affect work that has been already performed. This means rework costs for work that has already started or worse, been completed.
2. **Schedule:** With each scope change, precious project resources are diverted to activities that were not identified in the original project scope, leading to pressure on the project schedule. The project manager must also consider impact on the project's critical path.
3. **Quality:** When not analyzed thoroughly, scope changes lead to quick fixes that can affect product quality.
4. **Morale:** Scope changes can cause a loss of control of the team's planned work. Changing focus or direction to meet the change requests adversely impacts team morale.

The later a change is addressed, the greater the cost, risk and duration

Cost, Risk, Duration

Definition | Requirements | Conceptual Design | Detailed Design | Build | Testing | Definition | Live

WHEN SCOPE IS NOT MANAGED

What can happen when scope is not managed? These real-world examples illustrate the necessity of scope change management.

Case 1	Requirements documents are written and a project plan is created to produce a large Web-based product around core specifications. As the specifications are written and then reviewed, new faces are added to the committees and innocent statements emerge: "You know it will need to . . ." "Now, come to think of it . . ." and "By the way . . ." The specifications, written by several team members, begin undergoing rapid change. As a result of poor scope change management, the specifications contain conflicting and ambiguous statements. Integration issues arise, quality suffers and the cost rises. *The project manager needed to recognize that the comments from the new faces were more than minor details, they were scope changes. It would be appropriate to call a scope management meeting with the stakeholders to review a consolidated list of the comments.*
Case 2	A product selection project is undertaken based on an identified plan. In the initial project phase, the scope of user involvement is increased significantly and additional deliverables are identified. It is important to keep the project moving; therefore, the project schedule and budget are never revised, leading to significant delivery issues. *Scope should have been defined and reviewed with all stakeholders at every phase of the project. When the scope was increased, it should have been accompanied by change requests and proper status reporting and accounting.*

Case Study

A public sector organization had sub-contracted the development of a major new system to a software house. Progress was slow and both sides were raising many concerns. We were asked to investigate various problems that had been building up.

One area of concern was raised by the sub-contracting software house:

> *Changes—we have been inundated with changes. We've had to make thousands of changes to the design and it's almost impossible to get the client organization to recognize them or to allow for them in the planning and performance criteria.*

The client organization had a different view:

> *Changes—yes, there's been one change so far; and we're working on a second. It's not really a problem at all.*

To the client organization, a change meant, in effect, a formal re-negotiation of the contract—subject to the same extensive procedures as the original procurement contract. It would take months to approve a change request. To the software house, a change meant every instance where they were forced to change any completed element of the work due to some unavoidable problem with the original specifications. Given the enormous weight of the formal change approval process, it would be unrealistic to wait for formal approval except in the largest cases. What is worse, they probably would not get paid for those thousands of minor but essential changes.

Although it is not required for the Project Definition, this is a good time to establish the mechanism that will be used, particularly if it involves a system that needs to be selected, acquired and implemented. The Change Control system would normally be part of the same overall set of procedures and tools that will be used to support the other project management activities. A number of commercial software tools are available. It would also be straightforward to set up your own local system using client server or web technology. In relatively simple projects, standard tools such as e-mail and spreadsheets could meet the needs.

STARTING UP THE CHANGE CONTROL PROCESS

The Change Control process will involve a combination of procedures, responsibilities and systems. The key to success is to have a well-controlled but efficient process. Define and agree:

- On what basis changes should be approved,
- Who does what,
- The membership of the Change Control Board(s),
- The detailed procedures, forms, etc,
- Protocols for levels of authority, e.g. what types of change can be approved without reference to the project's business owners,
- Linkage to other management procedures, e.g. the issue management process, configuration management,
- Which tools will be used to support and manage the process,
- How to communicate and promote the process and its importance to all participants.

Here is an example process for dealing with issues:

Example Scope and Change Control Process

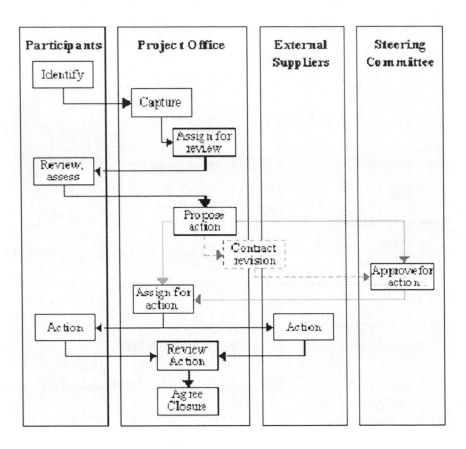

Any participant or other concerned party may raise Change Requests. The Project Office team and Project Manager will ensure they are captured and proactively manage them to conclusion.

An initial review should be made to examine the need for the change, how it could be achieved and what the consequences would be. The most appropriate member of the Project Team would normally perform this review. Based on those conclusions, the recommended action would be proposed.

In this example, there are three possible courses for the approval of the change:

- The Project Manager can approve minor changes within scope.
- Any change affecting an external sub-contractor would need to be reviewed with that contractor who would agree any necessary contract revisions or payments etc.
- Changes of scope and contract revisions would require the approval of the Steering Committee (or it might have been a Change Control Board).

In making the decision, the Project Manager, Change Control Board or Steering Committee would be guided by the pre-established principles for making change decisions.

After the action is agreed the Project Team and/or the external sub-contractor assign the work for action. When complete, the action would be reviewed and the Change Request closed. It is possible that the agreed action could have more than one stage. For example, it might be better to introduce a temporary solution so that the overall benefit from the project can be delivered, and then build a permanent solution after the system is live.

MANAGING SCOPE AND CHANGE REQUESTS DURING PROJECT

Not all changes follow the approved process. Often team members will be persuaded to make a change without using the approved procedure where it seems necessary but minor. Although this can seem practical to those concerned, it represents a risk to the project. The Project Manager and Project Office team should be alert for uncontrolled changes. Where necessary, changes should be painlessly re-directed into the correct procedure.

The Change Control process will run continuously during the project, and potentially beyond that into live running. The Project Office team and the Project Manager will administer and control the process.

In many ways the change request form is similar to the Issue Submission Form. The difference is that the Change Request addresses specific changes to be reviewed, authorized and made, whereas the Issue Submission Form captures less-well-defined information. In the Change Request there is more attention to the exact nature of the changes, whether they are scope changes, where they lie in the project lifecycle, which specific document or deliverable references need attention, etc.

Specific attention is paid to the cost and implications, identifying where work will be required and what its impact will be in terms of cost, risk and timescale. In particular, a benefit case will be prepared to summarize why the change should be made.

The Project Manager, Change Control Board or Steering Committee will use this Benefit Case in making a decision, in line with the pre-established guiding principles.

The status of the Change Request and its approval level should be tracked. In addition to the database of Change Requests, there would be logs and various management reports to allow the project leadership to track and control the changes. The Technical and administrative tracking of the actual changes would normally be made using the Configuration Management process.

At the End of the Phase

The Change Control process continues throughout the project, so no specific action is necessarily required at the end of each phase. Nevertheless, phase end is a good time to review the status of Change Requests, ensuring requests have been sanctioned in a timely fashion within the phase, and, in particular, allowing for their impact in the detailed planning for the following phase.

At the End of the Project

Some Change Requests may have been deferred for processing after the project is complete. This can be an easier option than disrupting the interrelated development and testing during the initial project. It might also be non-beneficial to delay the entire project to accommodate a change that could wait until benefit from the main functionality has been generated. At the end of the project, it is important that any outstanding actions are reviewed and the appropriate procedure is initiated to get them addressed. (It is easy to forget those promises after the project has finished.)

The Project Office should ensure all changes have been properly finalized. All Change Requests should either have been completed or passed onwards for subsequent processing. The permanent documentation and other deliverables (e.g. training) should have been updated to reflect the changes.

Change Requests may often reflect lessons to be learned for future projects. It is always worthwhile reviewing what can be learned and submitting any new knowledge or wisdom into the various knowledge repositories. Note, in particular, any situations where existing approaches or sample plans should be updated.

TOOLS AND TECHNIQUES FOR INTEGRATED CHANGE CONTROL

1) **Change control system**:—A change control system is a collection of formal, documented procedures that define how project performance will be monitored and evaluated, and includes the steps by which official project documents may be changed. It includes the paperwork, tracking systems, processes and approval levels necessary for authorizing changes.

2) **Configuration management**:—Configuration management is any documented procedures used to apply to technical and administrative directive, surveillance to:

  e. Identify and document the functional and physical characteristics of an item or system.
  f. Control any changes to such characteristics.
  g. Record and report the changes and its implementation status.
  h. Audit the items and systems to verify conformance to requirements.

3) **Performance measurement**:—Performance measurement techniques such as earned value help to assess whether variances from the plan require corrective action.

4) **Additional plan**:—Projects seldom run exactly according to plan. Prospective changes may require new or revised cost estimates, modified activity sequences, schedules, resources requirements, analysis of risk response alternatives, or other adjustments to the project plan.

5)   **Project management information system**:—PMIS consists of tools and techniques used to gather, integrate, and disseminate the outputs of project management processes. It is used to support all aspects of the project management from initiating through closing, and can include both manual and automated systems. Thus PMIS provides the means for achieving the measure-record-analyze-act system for ensuring the minimization of waste in the control system.

STAGE–GATE APPROACH TO PROJECT CONTROL

According to Harvey (1995), the stage-gate system involves the decision being made actively at each milestone, whether the project should continue. The criteria for passing the next stage must be laid down in advance. Calling a halt to activities can save future expenditure, and must never be discounted as an option, particularly where:

- The majority of the benefits from the activities have already been achieved by the organization.
- The initial plans and estimates have turned out to be wildly inaccurate.
- A new alternative which is more attractive has materialized.
- Organization strategy changes and the project outcome ceases to be in line with the new strategy.
- Key personnel leave the organization.
- The project requires a higher level; of capability than the organization possesses.
- To continue would endanger the organization financially as cash flow would be considerable.

The options include winding-up of the activities (which can often cause bad feelings amongst the project team and can lead to future disenchantment) or finding ways of maximizing the potential benefit whilst minimizing the risk or expenditure through taking in a partner or licensing another firm to run the project to completion.

EFFECTING CHANGE CONTROL

Project scope control changes are fed back through the planning process, technical and planning documents are updated as needed, and stakeholders are notified as appropriate. Actions taken include:

a) **Corrective action:**—taken to bring expected future project performance in line with the project plan.

b) **Documenting lessons learned:**—the causes of variance, the reasoning behind the corrective action chosen, and other types of lessons learned from the scope change control should be documented, so that this information becomes part of the historical database for both this project and other projects of the performing organization.

c) **Adjusted baseline:**—depending upon the nature of the change, the corresponding baseline document may be revised and reissued to reflect the approved change from the new baseline for future changes.

TIPS AND TECHNIQUES FOR EFFECTING CHANGE CONTROL

Here are helpful tips and techniques for keeping scope change on track:

1. **Proactive Change Identification:** Scope changes are waiting to happen, so the project manager should take an active role in identifying these changes with stakeholders. By being proactive, the project manager can incorporate the vital few changes that account for 80% of the stakeholders' issues and concerns.

2. **Sponsor Approval:** Always get the sponsor's approval and buy-in for the change request before authorizing any related work. If it is difficult to have the sponsor review every change, ask him/her to review a set of change requests. Alternatively,

the change can be classified as routine or in need of further analysis.

3. **Thorough Impact Analysis:** It's easy to conduct a superficial change impact analysis; however the repercussions are not very pleasant. An impact analysis needs to consider all the configuration items that will be affected by the change and associated costs.

4. **Communicate Changes:** In a large project team, changes can be overlooked if they are not communicated in a timely way. People like to know what they are working on and to be kept informed of project decisions. Proper team communications are essential to understanding and overcoming resistance to change.

5. **Avoid Scope Creep:** Scope creep occurs when changes are allowed without proper impact analysis, and without reviewing schedule and cost implications. This is common with repetitive minor incremental adjustments, where the project budget and schedule are not kept in sync with the effort involved for the changes. In this scenario, there is no way to avoid a runaway project syndrome. Scope creep is a symptom of a process problem; the solution is to implement a process to track each change and control its implementation.

Here is a sample Change Request Form.

Project R

Change Request Form

Demonstration Form Only - No Processing is Performed

Requested by: _____	Project area: [Project R ▼]
Job title: _____	Reference: [000001]
Contact number: _____	Date Reported: _____

Description

[_____]

Priority: [Low ▼] Issue cross reference: [000001] Affected components are: [Live ▼] [Submit]

Assessment:

Assigned to assessor: _____ Date: _____ Reference: component(s) affected

☐ Scope change   ☐ Programming
☐ Change to requirements   ☐ User documentation
☐ System design   ☐ Training
☐ Business process   ☐ Operational procedures

[_____]   [Submit]

Action(s):

Assigned to for action: _____ Date: _____

Action(s): [_____]   Impact: [_____]

External cross reference: _____ Benefit case: [_____]

Status: [Pending approval ▼]

Cost: _____   [Submit]

Outcome

[_____]

Closure approved by: _____ Closure date: _____

[Submit]

CHANGE CONTROL SHEET

Project Title		Project Number
Project Manager		
CHANGE REQUEST		
Originator Phone:	Date of request	Change request no. *allocated by Change Controller*
Items to be changed		Reference(s)
Description of change (reasons for change, benefits, date required)		
Estimated cost and time to implement (quotation attached? Yes No)		
Priority/Constraints (impact on other deliverables, implications of not proceeding, risks)		
CHANGE EVALUATION		
What is affected	Work required (resources, costs, dates)	
Related change requests		
Name of evaluator	Date evaluated	Signature
CHANGE APPROVAL		

Accepted Rejected Deferred	Name	Signed	Date
Comments			

CHANGE IMPLEMENTATION			
Asset	Implementer	Date completed	Signature

Change Control Log

Project Title	Project Number
Project Manager	

Change number	Description of change	Date received	Date evaluated	Date approved	Date completed

Performance Checklist

Intended use of this checklist

Used by a project team, quality assurance personnel, or project manager when reviewing measures of project performance

ID	Response	Items to Consider
1		Do actual trends correspond to planned trends? If not, is the variance within tolerances?
2		Is the variance approximately the same each reporting period?
3		Are actual values within planned limits?
4		Is there no evidence of outlying values and other anomalies affecting the results?
5		Are sources of any outlying values and other anomalies understood and under control?
6		Do multiple indicators lead to similar conclusions?
7		Is all other project information consistent with these results?

Project Monitoring Checklist

Intended use of this checklist:

For a project team and/or a Project Manager to evaluate the effectiveness of the project monitoring process. The checklist contains items to consider when checking the work of a project manager and project team in monitoring the project to its plan.

ID	Items to be Considered
1	Has the project plan been approved and the work started as planned?
2	Has the project been staffed to the level projected?
3	Are the key elements being monitored (at least weekly) to ensure that their progress is in accordance with their plan? Items that may be included: • Tasks starting and ending as planned • Deliverables with content and quality level required • Level of effort as planned • Milestones being met when planned • Critical project resources as planned • Risk management progress • Issues and action item resolution • Measures to handle key project issues
4	Is a change management activity being used to process changes?
5	Are action items being followed and tracked to closure?

6	Have weekly progress reports been sent to the team and Project Manager?
7	Has the project been monitoring for and reporting potential risks?
8	Has Quality Assurance been reviewing project work products and activities, identifying any exceptions to the project plan and/or organization processes?
9	Have the deviations (as identified by quality assurance) been reviewed, discussed and resolved with the project team and project manager?
10	Have the items that were not resolved been raised to management?
11	Have the items to be placed under configuration management been reviewed by the appropriate organizations?
12	Have all the items that were planned to be under configuration control been placed under configuration control?
13	Have the states of the various baselines been communicated to the appropriate people?
	Other?

Project archives:—a complete set of indexed project records should be prepared for archiving by the appropriate parties. Any project-specific or program wide historical data bases pertinent to the project should be updated. When projects are done under contract, or when they involve

The value of having a planned project termination is in leveraging all of the information and experience gathered throughout the project. If the solution is implemented and the team immediately disbands, you don't have an opportunity to wrap up the loose ends, do staff evaluations, document key learning or ensure that appropriate deliverables are transitioned to support. Whatever the reason for termination, there are key learning, team evaluations and other wrap-up activities that needs to be undertaken to make the most of what was done on the project

It is the responsibility of the project manager to build project termination activities into the project work plan. These should be seen as vital parts of the project, not an afterthought as the team is getting disbanded. The project is not considered completed until the termination activities are performed—just as it would not be complete without the implementation activities being finished.

APPROPRIATE PROJECT TERMINATION ACTIVITIES

When the project work plan is created, think about the activities that need to be performed to gracefully and appropriately terminate the project. These activities include:

I. Hold project conclusion meeting

A meeting should be held with the team, project sponsor and appropriate stakeholders to formally conclude the project. This project meeting will include stepping through a recap project, documenting things that went right and things that went wrong, strengths and weaknesses of the project and project management processes, and the remaining steps required to terminate the project. Techniques or processes that worked especially well, or especially poorly, are identified as key learnings of the project. If your organization has a way to publish or leverage these key learnings, they should be sent to the appropriate group. (Key learning that seems to work consistently on many projects, in many circumstances, might be raised to the level of a best practice and be utilized for all similar projects.)

An agenda for the conclusion meeting should focus on what the project was supposed to accomplish and what the project actually accomplished. The discussion should lead to a set of key learnings that describe what went well and what didn't work. The agenda would be as follows:

1. Discuss the purpose of the meeting
2. Develop ground rules (optional)
3. List what the project should have achieved.
4. Describe what the project actually achieved.
5. Discuss "why" for any discrepancies between "should do" and "actually did".
6. Agree on a set of lessons learned for future projects.
7. List and document any remaining work required to close the project. This includes activities such as those described below.

II. Declare success or failure

Sometimes it is obvious the project was completely successful and in other cases the project is a total failure. However, in many cases, there are mixed results. For instance, the major deliverables may have been completed, but the project was over budget. Or, the project team delivered on time and within budget, but the solution only met 80% of the business requirements. The key to declaring success is to define up-front what the success criteria are. If an agreement is reached with the sponsor and the appropriate functional manager on what success means, the project team can be evaluated against those criteria. The project should first rate itself against those criteria, and then take the recommendation to the sponsor for validation.

III. Transition the solution to support

If the solution will exist outside of the project, it should be transitioned to the appropriate support organization. The transition includes knowledge transfer to the support team, completion and turnover of all documentation, turnover of the list of remaining work, etc.

IV. Turnover Project Files

A discussion should take place with the support organization to determine which project and project management materials accumulated during the project that should be turned over to the support team. Based on this agreement, some of the project material may be deleted or destroyed, backed-up, archived, etc. Those files and documents needed by the support organization should be turned over to them to store in the appropriate long-term library or folders.

V. Conduct Performance Reviews

If the project was substantial, it may be appropriate to do performance reviews after the project completes. In this case, the project manager and the sponsor evaluate the entire project team. The project manager reviews the entire team or at least the direct reports. Sometimes the team is rated as a whole and then team members use the team rating as input into a personal performance review. Other times, the team members may have individual reviews based on only their own contributions. There should be some tie, however, between team and individual performance.

VI. Close all Contracts

Your project may have required the assistance of vendors for people, hardware, software, supplies, etc. Generally speaking, these project—specific contracts should be closed as a part of terminating the project. Of course, some contracts are broader than your project and these will remain open. You may have an open contract with a consulting firm, for instance, and you may have opened a Statement of Work for the specific services provided on your project. In that case, the general contract would remain open, but the specific statement of work would be closed. It is also very likely that all invoices have not been paid (or even submitted) when the project officially ends. However, the project manager or the appropriate contracts administrator should be responsible for closing these project specific contracts after all outstanding bills have been paid (Settle outstanding accounts receivable and payable).

VII. Reassign the remaining Project Team

Any remaining team members should be reassigned when all the termination activities are completed. For some people, this may mean completely new projects. For contract people, it may mean the end of their assignments. For part-timers, it may mean a return to their other full-time role. Some team members may transition into the support organization to continue working on this same solution.

Guidelines and Practices

It is often said that doctors have a terrible time talking to patients and their families where terminal illness is concerned. Doctors, by definition, are dedicated to wellness. They prefer to focus on making people well and in preserving a healthy state. So, in the case of the eventual termination of their patient's life, they make every attempt (perhaps subconsciously) to distance themselves from the situation and all involved.

This is not unlike the situation of project termination. Whether normal termination or abnormal, the typical project manager and project team will do everything in their power to avoid the subject and to distance themselves from the situation.

In the case of normal termination, the motivation is three-fold. First, the thought of leading the initiation of a new project is much more exciting than doing cleanup work on the project that is nearing completion. Certainly, it is much more interesting to move to the initiation phase of a new project than to manage the mundane details of cleaning up the odds and ends of the project approaching completion. Frankly, most people would find this phase to be boring. Second, project participants are on the lookout for new project opportunities, recognizing that their current assignment is coming to an end.

Third, many projects are delivered late, over budget, and with less scope than originally designed. Who wants to be around when the blame is allocated? In the case of pre-completion termination, we have to deal with the psychology of failure. There is a prevalent stigma that the project that does not reach satisfactory completion is a failed Project. Therefore, the thought of premature termination is purged from our minds, as we blindly forge ahead with what may be, in reality, a failed project.

Considering abnormal termination is a bit like dealing with risk. Often, we resist performing a risk evaluation because we may find that there is a potential downside and we have difficulty facing such negative aspects of the project. For most of us, it is heretical to consider cutting a project short of its planned conclusion. Saving face becomes preferable to making a profit or satisfying a client. Nevertheless, there are times when it becomes prudent to end a project short of its normal completion.

Experience has shown us that it makes sense to have a set of guidelines and practices for each phase of a project. The termination phase is no exception. We proceed here with a punch list of the typical activities associated with bringing a project to a clean close.

This is a phase that we usually let get away. Everyone who has been on the project is busy patting themselves on the back (for achieving project success), looking for new challenges, or running for cover (if the project has failed). In doing so, we lose a lot of valuable data and experience. There is much to do to tidy up the loose ends, capture lessons learned, and document new technology and capabilities. A key benefit from doing projects and managing them well through to closeout is derived from technology transfer and the final project audit.

ACTIVITIES IN CLOSEOUT PHASE

- The Project Audit (This can also be performed at key stages during the project execution)
- Why, What, When, Who
- Current status of project
- Forecasts
- Status of key items
- Risk assessment
- Info pertinent to other projects
- Recommendations
- Post-Mortem (Evaluation)
- Scope Accomplished
- Technical Objectives Met
- Recommendations for other projects
- Project Historical Data
- Other Close-out Items
- Final Measurements
- Punch List
- Uncompleted tasks
- Special Close-out Tasks
- Final Report
- Client Acceptance
- Client Acceptance Documents
- Client Feedback
- Testimonials
- Assets Disposition

- Personnel Disposition and Reports
- Sell/Transfer/Toss Residuals
- Arrange for transfer or reassignment of dedicated resources
- Release assigned resources
- Document Transactions
- Document performance
- "atta-boy/atta-girl" letters
- Archives

While terminating a project before its normal completion could often be called a failed project, this is not always the case. When it becomes evident that the project objectives cannot be satisfactorily met, it often makes sense to reach a negotiated closure. The key operative here is "negotiated". An aborted project generally means a loss for most stakeholders. Just about everyone ends up with less than they had expected from the successfully completed project. So now, the objective is to preserve as much of the planned gains, for all involved, with some balance for all stakeholders.

REASONS FOR STOPPING IN MID-STREAM

In the words of Kenny Rogers' popular song, we need to **"know when to hold them and when to fold them."** The general basis for early termination is that the project cannot meet the stated objectives, and to continue to pursue these objectives will do more damage than bringing the project to an immediate end. There can be a multitude of reasons for such actions. For example:

- Product (development) failed to achieve goal
- Drug development failed in testing
- Material development did not meet expectations
- Window of opportunity has passed
- Competitors have beaten you to the punch

- Potential client has found another source
- Technology/market has changed
- The new transcontinental railroad makes your plans for a new line of stage coaches obsolete
- Technology failed or became obsolete during project execution
- You're developing a new strain of mules when Robert Fulton appears on the scene
- Your software development methodology can't support the capability goals
- You're developing a new type of razor strop when Gillette introduces the safety razor
- Economics of the project changed
- Market test sample for proposed new periodical fails to meet 1% economic feasibility test
- Target client would not accept product
- Client has chosen a different supplier
- Costs have gone up e.g. the production of the Yellow Brand size D-Eveready Battery was stopped because of high production costs.
- Original economic analysis was flawed
- Project performance is so off the mark as to make it impossible to reasonably deliver
- Better alternative to meet primary goal makes current project unnecessary
- Cannot complete project in time to meet iron-clad deadline
- Your new Christmas card design cannot be completed until late December.
- Cannot meet quality objectives
- The test yield of new super-fast chips is below the 25% acceptance level
- Projected cost of field modifications exceeds planned profits
- Client/sponsor is no longer interested
- Project is hurting other work of the firm

- Your firm has limited resources and a large portfolio of projects. An evaluation indicates that other projects that offer a greater return or a better alignment with corporate goals can't get started because key resources are committed to the current project.
- Partners or suppliers can't hold up their end
- Can't get the proper resources/skills
- You're building tract houses and you can't get framers
- An outbreak of war shuts off your supply of raw materials

Certainly, early termination is not something that we regularly seek or something that we accept without careful consideration of the consequences. On the other hand, we should not close our mind to such options.

> *Project goals can be better achieved by outsourcing the project. Covered in the list, above, are wide ranges of issues, including schedule, resources, costs, profits, technical objectives, quality, marketing, and health of the firm. As part of the normal set of project management practices, progress toward all of these objectives should be regularly examined and evaluated. Part of that evaluation should be consideration of early project termination. We need to be prepared to ask: "What if we ended this project now? Would most of the stakeholders be better off than if we tried to keep things going?"*

EARLY TERMINATION ANALYSES

The potential consideration of early termination should be based on an examination of current and projected performance against the project objectives. If it is determined that any of these performance items will be significantly deficient, then we analyze the impact of the penalties or losses associated with terminating the project against those that we can expect from trying to bring the project to its designed completion.

Paramount in this analysis is an evaluation of the impact on the stakeholders' satisfaction. In some cases, the decision (to terminate early) will be a no-brainer. It will be based on a clear indication that there will be no benefits from beating a dead horse. In other instances, the decision will be less clear, often leading us to continue a flawed project to a lingering death.

People need to be willing to accept a "cut our losses" decision. This acceptance can only be accomplished through the presentation of a revised business case that clearly demonstrates the newly evaluated factors.

The process for early termination is essentially the same as for normal termination. To the list presented earlier, we should add the following:

1. Evaluate ways to save the maximum benefits from the work already done
2. Evaluate the potential to create a new, revised project from the remains of the current one
3. Negotiate revised set of project financials, based on what actually was accomplished or delivered
4. Identify what went wrong that necessitated early termination and record this as "lessons learned"

MODES OF PROJECT CLOSURE/TERMINATION

Project closure is a process that occurs whether a project is successful or not. The aim of the closure process is to cease the project at all levels with minimum administrative dislocation. The closure process is heavily influenced by the Parent Organization's Structure

The various types of project termination are:

Normal—A project that ends normally is the one that is completed as planned.

Premature—A project may be pushed to complete early even though the system may not include all of the envisioned features or functionality.

Perpetual—Some projects seem to take on a "life of their own" and are known as runaway or perpetual projects.

Failed—Unsuccessful project

Changed Priority—Financial or economic reasons may dictate that resources are no longer available to the project.

Project Termination Modes

According to Pinto (2007) there are four chief modes of project termination:

1. Termination by extinction (by decision) occurs when:

- It has successfully completed its scope that has been accepted by the Client
- It has failed
- It has been superseded by external developments
- It no longer has sufficient Support of Senior Management

2. Project termination by extension is where though the technical processes of the project are immediately terminated there are still management processes to be planned and executed by the project manager

- Project Team members reassigned or released
- Project materials and equipment disbursed
- Preparation of final reports and reviews

3. Project termination by addition concludes a project by institutionalizing it as part of the parent organization (in-house successfully completed project).

- Personnel, property and equipment are transferred to newly created organizational unit within parent organization

4. Project termination by integration occurs when the project's resources, as well as deliverables are integrated into operations of client or parent company

- Project personnel, property and equipment are reintegrated within the organization's existing structures.
- Personnel released from the project assignment are reabsorbed within their functional departments to perform other duties, or wait for new project assignments.
- Project Manager must plan/execute smooth integration and termination process
- Most common mode and most complex for Project Manager

5. Project Termination by starvation can happen for a number of reasons:

- There may be political reasons for keeping a project officially 'on the books' even though the organization does not intend it to succeed or anticipate it will ever be finished.
- The project may have a powerful sponsor who must be placated with the maintenance of his or her 'pet project'.

- Due to budget cuts, an organization may keep a project in the files but reactivate them when the economic situation improves.

Project Termination Supervision

Should the Project Manager Supervise Termination?

- Depends on potential or reluctance to terminate
- Is the Project Manager required for transition or integration?
  - Will another member of the project team do?

Some organizations use specialist termination managers thereby releasing the Project Manager for other projects as soon as possible.

Termination Manager

Termination is a long and complicated process. Like any other project life cycle, termination planning aims at increasing the project's probability of success. Shtub, Bard and Globerson (2005), hold that once the management has approved cancellation, the following actions should be taken:

1. Set project termination milestones
2. Establish termination phase target costs and budget allocation.
3. Specify major milestone deliveries.
4. Define organizational structure and workforce after termination.

Post Implementation Audit

Establish the true status of the project with respect to its planned status (If implementation has occurred the planned status project objective' is achieved)

PROJECT DISPOSITION PHASE—THE CASE OF AN IT SYSTEM

THE OBJECTIVE OF PROJECT DISPOSITION PHASE

The Disposition Phase will be implemented to eliminate a large part of a system or as in most cases, close down a system and end the life cycle process. The system in this phase has been declared surplus and/or obsolete and will be scheduled for shutdown. The emphasis of this phase will be to ensure that data, procedures, and documentation are packaged and archived in an orderly fashion, making it possible to reinstall and bring the system back to an operational status, if necessary, and to retain all data records in accordance with policies regarding retention of electronic records.

The Disposition Phase represents the end of the project life cycle. A Disposition Plan shall be prepared to address all facets of archiving, transferring, and disposing of the project and data. Particular emphasis shall be given to proper preservation of the data processed by the project so that it is effectively migrated to another project or archived in accordance with applicable records management regulations and policies for potential future access. The project disposition activities preserve information not only about the current project but also about the evolution of the project through its life cycle.

1. Tasks and Activities

The objectives for all tasks identified in this phase are to retire the project systems, software, hardware and data. The tasks and activities actually performed are dependent on the nature of the project. The disposition activities are performed at the end of the systems life cycle. The disposition activities ensure the orderly termination of the system and preserve vital information about the system so that some or all of it may be reactivated in the future if necessary. Particular emphasis shall be given to proper preservation of the data processed by the system, so that the data are effectively migrated to another system or disposed of in accordance with applicable records management and programme area regulations and policies for potential future access. These activities may be expanded, combined or deleted, depending on the size of the system.

2. Prepare Disposition Plan

The Disposition Plan must be developed and implemented. The Disposition Plan will identify how the termination of the system /data will be conducted, and when, as well as the system termination date, software components to be preserved, data to be preserved, disposition of remaining equipment, and archiving of life-cycle products.

3. Archive or Transfer Data

The data from the old system will have to be transferred into the new system or if it is obsolete, archived.

4. Archive or Transfer Software Components

Similar to the data that is archived or transferred, the software components will need to be transferred to the new system, or if that is not feasible, disposed of.

5. Archive Life Cycle Deliverables

- A lot of documentation went into developing the application or system. This documentation needs to be archived, where it can be referenced if needed at a later date.
- End the project in an orderly manner
- Follow the Disposition Plan for the orderly breakdown of the project, its components and the data within.

Dispose of equipment

- If the equipment can be used elsewhere in the organization, recycle. If it is obsolete, notify the property management office to excess all hardware components.

6. Conduct Post—Termination Review

This review will be conducted at the end of the Disposition Phase and again within 6 months after disposition of the system by the project manager.

ROLES AND RESPONSIBILITIES DURING THE DISPOSITION PHASE

1. **Project Manager.** The project manager is responsible and accountable for the successful execution of the Disposition Phase activities.
2. **Data Administrator.** The Disposition Plan may direct that only certain systems data be archived. The Data Administrator would identify the data and assist technical personnel with the actual archive process. The Data Administrator may be involved with identifying data, which due to its sensitive nature must be

destroyed. They would also be involved with identifying and migrating data to a new or replacement system.

3. **Security Managers**. The security managers will need to make sure that all access authority has been eliminated for the users. Any users that only use the application should be removed from the system while others that use other applications as well as this one may still need access to the overall system, but not the application being shut-down. If there is another application that is taking the place of this application, the security managers should coordinate with the new security managers.

DELIVERABLES DURING THE DISPOSITION PHASE

The following deliverables are initiated and finalized during the Disposition Phase

1. Disposition Plan

The objectives of the plan are to end the operation of the system in a planned, orderly manner and to ensure that system components and data are properly archived or incorporated into other systems. This will include removing the active support by the operations and maintenance organizations. The users will need to play an active role in the transition. All concerned groups will need to be kept informed of the progress and target dates. The decision to proceed with Disposition will be based on recommendations and approvals from an In-Process review or based on a date (or time period).

This plan will include a statement of why the application is no longer supported, a description of replacement / upgrade, list of tasks/ activities (transition plan) with estimated dates of completion and the notification strategy. Additionally, it will include the responsibilities for future residual support issues such as identifying media alternatives if technology changes; new software product transition plans and alternative support issues (once the application is removed); parallel operations of retiring and the new software product; archiving of the software product, associated documentation, movement of logs, code; and accessibility of archive, data protection identification, and audit applicability.

2. Post-Termination Review Report

A report at the end of the process that details the findings of the Disposition Phase Review. It includes details of where to find all products and documentation that has been archived.

3. Archived System

The packaged set of data and documentation containing the archived application.

4. Issues for Consideration

Update of Security plans for archiving and the contingency plans to reestablish the system should be in place.

All documentation about the application, system logs and configuration will be archived along with the data and a copy of the Disposition Plan.

5. Phase review activity

The Post-Termination Review shall be performed after the end of this final phase. This phase-end Review shall be conducted within six months after disposition of the system. The Post-Termination Report documents the lessons learned from the shutdown and archiving of the terminated system.

FINAL PROJECT REPORT

The final project report should be a repository of wisdom gained. It is a commentary not an evaluation

- ◦ Recommend and justify changes to current practices
- ◦ Draw attention to practices that worked unusually well

Final Report: Some Headings

a) **Project Summary**
- • Project description, Scope, schedule, budget, and quality objectives

b) **Project Performance**
- • Compare proposed to post implementation audit
- • Comment on deviations experienced

c) **Administrative Performance**
- • Outline administrative performance
- • Oversee final disposition

d) **Organizational structure**
- • How did the structure impede or speedup operations?

e) **Project and administrative teams**
- • Confidential comments on performance of individuals and teams in the project.

f) **Techniques of Project Management**
- • Planning, estimating, budgeting, scheduling, resource allocation and control

MID-TERM EVALUATION REPORT: SAMPLE OUTLINE

A mid-term evaluation is conducted for an ongoing programme or project. It serves two immediate purposes: decision-making and taking stock of initial lessons from experience. Specifically, a mid-term evaluation provides a programme or project manager with a basis for identifying appropriate actions to:

a) Address particular issues or problems in design, implementation and management, and
b) Reinforce initiatives that demonstrate the potential for success.

Capacity Development Project Evaluation

A capacity development project aims to develop the abilities of individuals and institutions, individually and collectively, to carry out development tasks. It has four interrelated dimensions: individual learning, organizations, organizational interrelationships and enabling environment.

This section contains an outline, in question form, of the report for a mid-term evaluation of a capacity development project. The questions may be modified or new ones may be added depending on the specific characteristics of the project and the purposes of the evaluation. In this sense, the outline is a guide, not a blueprint.

Executive Summary

- What are the context and purpose of the evaluation?
- What are the main conclusions, recommendations and lessons learned?

Introduction

- Whose decision was it to evaluate the project?
- What is the purpose of the evaluation? Is there any special reason why the evaluation is being done at mid-term and not at, or after, project completion?
- What products are expected from the evaluation?
- How will the evaluation results be used?
- What are the key issues addressed by the evaluation?
- What was the methodology used for the evaluation?
- What is the structure of the evaluation report? (How is the content organized?)

The Project and its Development Context

- When did the project start and what is its duration? What are the problems that the project seeks to address?
- What are the immediate and development objectives of the project?
- Who are the main stakeholders?
- What results are expected?

Findings and Conclusions

Project Concept and Design

Did the project document (i.e. the most recent approved version) clearly define the:

- problem to be addressed by the project, taking into account the institutional, socio-political, economic and environmental contexts as well as gender considerations?
- project approach or strategy?

- linkages among objectives, inputs, activities, outputs, expected outcomes and impact?
- implementation and management arrangements?
- indicators for use in monitoring and evaluation, differentiated by gender as applicable?

How relevant is the project to:

- o development priorities of the programme beneficiaries at the level being targeted (local or national, macro or sectoral), specifically in terms of capacity development?
    - Was the project designed to support the community's objective of establishing or enhancing the enabling environment to promote the development of a particular target group, geographic area or sector?
- o Donor areas of thematic focus (i.e., poverty eradication and sustainable livelihoods, gender in development, environmental and natural resource sustainability, and sound governance)?
    - Was the project designed to strengthen the capacities of relevant government agencies, private sector entities or civil society organizations to initiate and sustain development initiatives in these areas?
- o Donor comparative advantage vis-à-vis other donor agencies and development partners?
    - Was the project designed to capitalize on donor expertise and experience in capacity development at the particular level of intervention and areas of focus described above?
- o Needs of the direct beneficiaries, i.e., institutions and/ or individuals who are the direct recipients of technical cooperation aimed at strengthening their capacity to undertake development tasks that are directed at specific target groups?
    - Was the project designed to address specific issues relating to individual learning, organizational structures,

processes, management systems, networking and linkages that affect the performance of the direct beneficiaries?

- Were gender considerations taken into account in designing the project's strategy to address these issues?
- Did the direct beneficiaries participate in designing the project? If yes, what were the nature and extent of their participation?

Project Implementation

- **Efficiency**
  - How well has the project used its resources to produce target outputs?
  - How adequate are the quantity and quality of project inputs relative to the target outputs?
  - To what extent are local expertise (by gender) and indigenous technologies and resources used?
- **Effectiveness**
  - What is the project status with respect to target outputs in terms of quantity, quality and timeliness? What factors impede or facilitate the production of such outputs?
  - How useful are the outputs to the needs of the direct beneficiaries? Is there general acceptance of the outputs by these beneficiaries? Is there a significant gender differentiation in the usefulness of the outputs to direct beneficiaries?
  - Do the outputs contribute to the achievement of the immediate objectives of the project? What signs indicate this? Are monitoring and evaluation indicators appropriate or is there a need to establish or improve these indicators?

- **Implementation and management arrangements of the project**
  - How appropriate are the execution and implementation modalities?
  - How well is the project managed?
  - How adequate are monitoring and reporting mechanisms?
  - How adequate is the support provided by the donor agency office?
  - How effective are support-cost arrangements, if any, with donor agencies?
  - Do stakeholders, particularly the direct beneficiaries, participate in the management of the project? If yes, what are the nature and extent of their participation, by gender?
- **Areas for corrective action**
  - What problems in project implementation need to be resolved?
  - What are the flaws, if any, in design, implementation, monitoring and evaluation?
- **Areas of potential success**
  - Are there early indications of potential success?

Project Results

- Given the indicators established by the project and/or recommended by the evaluation team:
  - How has the project contributed to the development of the capacity of the direct beneficiaries to carry out their tasks in an environment of change in terms of (a) individual learning, by gender, and (b) improving organizational structures and interrelationships?
  - What is the likely impact of the project beyond the direct beneficiaries?

- ° Are there any signs of a potential contribution to the enabling environment or to the broader development context (i.e., institutional, socio-political, economic and environmental)?
- What factors affect the implementation of the project?
  - ° Is there adequate government commitment to the project?
  - ° Do the stakeholders have a sense of ownership of the project?
  - ° Have mechanisms been put in place to ensure the sustainability of project results?

Recommendations

- What corrective actions are recommended for the design, implementation, monitoring and evaluation of the project?
- What actions are recommended to follow up or reinforce initial benefits from the project?

Lessons Learned

- What are the main lessons that can be drawn from the project experience that may have generic application? What are the best and worst practices in formulating, implementing, monitoring and evaluating a capacity development project?

Annexes

- TOR; Itinerary ; List of persons interviewed
- Summary of field visits
- List of documents reviewed
- Questionnaire used and summary of results
- Any other relevant material

ANNUAL PROGRAMME/PROJECT REPORT

Purpose

The annual programme/project report (APR) is designed to obtain the independent views of the main stakeholders of a programme or project on its relevance, performance and the likelihood of its success. The main stakeholders are the target groups, programme or project management, the key agency responsible for the programme or project, and the sponsors.

The APR aims to:

- provide a rating and textual assessment of the progress of a programme or project in achieving its objectives;
- present stakeholders' insights into issues affecting the implementation of a programme or project and their proposals for addressing those issues; and
- serve as a source of inputs into the preparation of the annual report, a formal means of communication between the agency offices and headquarters through which agency experiences are captured for consolidation and dissemination to the development community.

The questions on relevance are meant to determine the extent to which the objectives and target groups of the programme or project remain valid and pertinent as originally planned or as subsequently modified owing to changing circumstances within the immediate context and the external environment of the programme or project. The questions about performance pertain to effectiveness, efficiency and timeliness. The questions on success focus on the potential impact, sustainability of results and contribution to capacity development of the programme or project.

Annual Programme/Project Report Template

Basic Programme/Project Information (To be provided by programme/project management)

Programme/project number and title: _____

Executing agency: _____

Project starting date

Originally planned: _____ Actual: _____

Project completion date

Originally planned: _____ Actual: _____

Total budget (KShs.): _____

Originally: _____ Latest signed revision: _____

Period covered by the report: _____

Date of tripartite/bipartite review (Indicate if planned or actual): _____

PART I. Numerical Rating

Rate the relevance and performance of the programme or project using the following scale:

Rate the relevance and performance of the programme or project using the following scale:

1. Highly Satisfactory
2. Satisfactory
3. Unsatisfactory with some positive elements
4. Unsatisfactory
5. Not applicable

Place your answers in the column that corresponds to your role in the programme or project.

Substantive Focus	Target Group(s)	Programme or Project manager	Agency	Sponsor
Relevance				
1. How relevant is the programme or project to the development priorities of the area?				

2. How relevant is the programme or project to the promotion of sustainable human development?			
3. Are appropriate beneficiary groups being targeted by the programme or project?			
4. Does the programme or project address the gender-differentiated needs of the target groups?			
5. Given the objectives of the programme or project, are the appropriate institutions being assisted?			
Performance			

1. Using the following indicators, rate the contribution of the outputs to the achievement of the immediate objectives:				
a. (Indicator 1)				
b. (Indicator 2)				
c. (Indicator 3)				
2. Rate the production of target outputs.				
3. Are the management arrangements of the programme or project appropriate?				
4. Are programme or project resources (financial, physical and manpower) adequate in terms of:				
a. quantity?				
b. quality?				

5. Are programme or project resources being used efficiently to produce planned results?				
6. Is the programme or project cost-effective compared to similar interventions?				
7. Based on its work plan, how would you rate the timeliness of the programme or project in terms of:				
a. production of outputs and initial results?				
b. inputs delivery?				

* Prior to the distribution of the form, the indicators must be listed, as reflected in the programme support document or project document or as agreed on by the stakeholders.

Please indicate your overall rating of the programme or project using the following letters:

A. Highly satisfactory
B. Satisfactory
C. Unsatisfactory, with some positive elements
D. Unsatisfactory
E. Not applicable

Substantive Focus	Target Group(s)	Programme or Project manager	Agency	Sponsor
Overall rating of the programme or project				

Explain the basis of your rating, which need not be limited to, or which may be different from, the relevance and performance criteria rated above. For the last year of the programme or project, the overall rating should include an assessment of the potential success of the programme or project as well as its relevance and performance.

Answer questions 1-8 <u>every year except the last year</u> of the programme or project.

Answer questions 9-14 <u>only for the last year</u> of the programme or project.

PART II. Textual Assessment

1. What are the major achievements of the programme or project vis-à-vis its objectives during the year under review?
2. What major issues and problems are affecting the implementation of the programme or project?
3. How should these issues or problems be resolved? Please explain in detail the action(s) recommended. Specify who should be responsible for such actions. Also indicate a tentative time frame and the resources required.
4. What are the potential areas for programme or project success? Please explain in detail in terms of potential impact, sustainability of results and contribution to capacity development.
5. What actions would you recommend to ensure that this potential for success translates into actual success?
6. What are the views of the target groups with regard to the programme or project? Please note any significant gender-based differences in those views.
7. To date, what lessons (both positive and negative) can be drawn from the experience of the programme or project?
8. If the programme or project has been evaluated, what is the implementation status of the recommendations made by the evaluators?
9. What are the major achievements of the programme or project vis-à-vis its objectives? Please explain them in detail in terms of potential impact, sustainability of results and contribution to capacity development?
10. What factors affected the implementation of the programme or project?
11. What lessons (both positive and negative) can be drawn from the experience of the programme or project?
12. What are the views of the target groups with regard to the programme or project? Please note any significant gender-based differences in those views.

13. If the programme or project has been evaluated, what is the implementation status of the recommendations made by the evaluators?
14. What activities or steps do you recommend as follow-up to the project?

_____

Rater's Name, Title, Organization Represented, Signature,

_____

Date

_____

Rater's Name, Title, Organization Represented, Signature

_____

Date

_____

Rater's Name, Title, Organization Represented, Signature

Date

_____

Rater's Name, Title, Organization Represented, Signature

_____

Date

CHAPTER FIVE

PROJECT COMMUNICATION

INTRODUCTION

Project communications management includes the processes required to ensure timely and appropriate generation, collection, dissemination, storage and ultimate disposition of project information. It provides the critical links among the people, ideas, and information that are necessary for success. Project communication entails the following:

a) *Communications planning*—determining the information and communications needs of the stakeholders: who needs what information, when they will need it, and how it will be given to them.

b) *Information distribution*—making needed information available to project stakeholders in a timely manner.

c) *Performance reporting*—collecting and disseminating performance information. This includes status reporting, progress measurement, and forecasting.

d) *Administrative closure*—generating, and disseminating information to formalize a phase in a timely manner.

Patrick Gudda

COMMUNICATION PLANNING

COMMUNICATION REQUIREMENTS

Communication requirements are the sum total of the information requirements of the stakeholders. Requirements are defined by combining the type and format of information required with an analysis of the value of that information. Information typically required to determine project communications requirement include:

1. Project organization and stakeholder responsibility relationship. discipline, departments and specialists involved in the project,
2. Logistics of how many individuals will be involved will be involved with the project and at which locations.
3. External information needs e.g. communicating with the media.

COMMUNICATION TECHNOLOGY

Communication technology or method used to transfer information back and forth among project stakeholders can vary significantly: from brief conversations to extended meetings; from simple written documents to immediately accessible online schedules and databases.

Communication technology factors that may affect the project include:

The immediacy for the need for information—is project success dependent upon having frequently updated information available on a moment's notice, or would regularly issued written reports suffice?

The availability of technology—are the systems that are already in placer appropriate, or do project needs warranty change?

The expected project staffing—are the proposed communication systems compatible with the expertise and experience of the project participants, or will extensive training and learning be required?

The length of the project—is the available technology likely to change before the project is over?

CONSTRAINTS

Constraints are factors that will limit the project management team's options, for example, if substantial project resources will be procured, more consideration will need to be given to handling contract information.

ASSUMPTIONS

Assumptions are factors for planning purposes, are considered to be true, real or certain. Assumptions affect all aspects of project planning, and are part of the progressive elaboration of the project. Project teams frequently identify, document, and validate assumptions as part of their planning process. For example, if the date a key person will become available is uncertain, the team may assume a specific start date. Assumptions generally involve some degree of risks.

COMMUNICATIONS MANAGEMENT PLAN

Communications management plan is a document that provides:

1. A collection and filling structure that details what methods will be used to gather and store various types of information. Procedures should also cover collecting and disseminating updates and corrections to previously distributed material.

2. Distributions structure that detail to whom information (status reports, data, schedule, technical documentation, .etc) will flow, and what methods (written, schedule, meetings, etc) will be used to distribute various types of information. The structure must be compatible with the responsibilities and reporting relationships described by the organization chart.

3. A description of information to be distributed, including format, content, level of detail, and conventions / definitions to be used.

4. Production schedules showing when each type of communication will be produced.

Methods of accessing information between schedules.

A method for updating and refining the communications management plan as the project progresses and develops.

TOOLS AND TECHNIQUES FOR INFORMATION DISTRIBUTION

Communication Skills

Communication skills are used to exchange information. The sender is responsible for making the information clear, unambiguous and complete, so that the receiver can receive it correctly, and for confirming that it is properly understood. The receiver is responsible for making sure that the information is received at its entirety and understood correctly. Communicating has many dimensions:

1. Written and oral, listening and speaking.
2. Internal (within the project) and external to the customers, the media, the public, etc).

3. Formal (reports, briefings, etc) and informal (memos, *ad hoc* conversations, etc)
4. Vertical (up and down the organization) and horizontal (with peers).

Information Retrieval System

Information retrieval systems would include manual filing systems, electronic data bases, project management software, and systems that allow access to technical documentation such as engineering drawings, design specifications, test plans etc.

Information Distribution Methods

Project information may be distributed using a variety of methods such as project meetings, hard-copy documents distribution, and shared access to networked databases, fax, electronic mail, voice mail, videoconferencing, and project in trainer.

PERFORMANCE REPORTING

Performance reporting involves collecting and disseminating performance information to provide stakeholders with information about how resources are being used to achieve project objectives. This process includes:

a) *Status reporting*—describing where the project now stands—for example, status related to schedule and budget metrics.
b) *Progress reporting*—describing what the project team has accomplished—for example, percent complete to schedule, or what is completed verses what is in process.
c) *Forecasting*—predicting future project status and progress.

Performance reporting should generally provide information on scope, schedule, cost and quality. Many projects also require information on risk and procurement. Reports may be prepared comprehensively or on an exception basis.

TOOLS AND TECHNIQUES FOR PERFORMANCE REPORTING

Performance reviews:—performance reviews are meetings held to assess project status and or progress. Performance reviews are typically used in conjunction with one or more of the performance-reporting techniques reported below.

Variance analysis:—variance analysis involves comparing actual project results to planned or expected results. Cost and schedule variances are the most frequently analyzed, but variances from plan in the areas of scope, resource, quality, and risk are often of equal or greater importance.

Trend analysis:—Trend analysis involves examining project results over time to determine if performance

Earned value analysis:—EVA in its various forms is the most commonly used method of performance measurement. It integrates scope, cost (or resource) and schedule measures to help the project management team assess project performance. EVA involves calculating three key areas for each activity.

The planned value (PV), previously called the budgeted cost of work schedule (BCWS), is that portion of the approved cost estimate planned to be spent on the activity during a given period.

The actual cost (AC), previously called the actual cost of work performed (ACWP), is the total of costs incurred in accomplishing work on the activity during a given period. This actual cost must correspond to whatever that was budgeted for the PV and the EV (example: direct hours only, direct costs only or all costs including direct costs).

The EV, previously called the budgeted cost of work performed (BCWP), is the value of the work actually completed.

These three values are used in combination to provide measures of whether or not work is being accomplished as planned. The most commonly used measures are:

- o the cost of variance, CV = EV-AC
- o schedule variance, SV = EV-PV

These two values, the CV and SV, can be converted to efficiency indicators to reflect the cost and schedule performance of any project.

The cost performance index (CPI = EV/ AC) is the most commonly cost-efficiency indicator.

The cumulative CPI (the sum of all individual EV budgets divided by the sum of all individual ACs) is widely used to forecast project cost at completion.

Also, the schedule performance index (SPI = EV / PV) is sometimes used in conjunction with the CPI to forecast the project completion estimates.

INFORMATION DISTRIBUTION TOOLS AND TECHNIQUES

Performance reports are distributed using the tools and techniques described earlier.

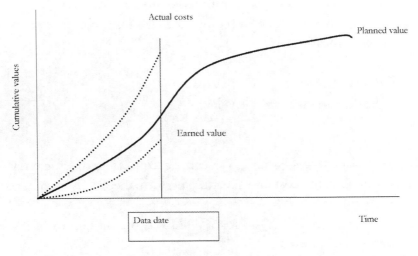

Illustrative graphic performance report

This S-curve displays cumulative EV analysis data.

Illustrative tabular performance report

WBS Element	Planned Budget	Earned Value (EV)	Cost Actual Cost (AC)	Cost Variance EV—AC	(CV/AC)	Schedule Variance EV-PV	SV-PV	Performance index WBS Element	Budget
Pre-pilot plan	68, 000	58,000	62,500	-4,500	-7.8	-5,000	-7.9	0.93	0.92
Checklists	64, 000	48,000	46, 800	1, 200	2.5	-16,000	-25.0	1.03	0.75
Curriculum	23, 000	20,000	23,500	-3,500	-17.5	-3,000	-13.0	0.85	0.87
Mid-term evaluation / Implementation support	60, 000	68,000	72,500	-4 500	-6.6	-2000	0.0	0.94	1.00
Manual of practice	12. 000	10,000	10,000	0	0.0	-800	-16.7	1.00	0.83
Roll-out plan	7, 000	6, 200	6, 000	200	3.2		-11.4	1.03	0.89
TOTAL	20, 000	13 500	18,000	-4600	-34.1	-6, 500	-32.5	0.75	0.68
	257, 000	223,700	234, 400	-16, 700	-7.0	-33, 300	-13.0	0.93	0.87

Source: Adapted from the *PMBOK* (2000) Edition p. 124

Performance reports organize and summarize the information gathered and present the results of any analysis. Reports should provide the kinds of information and the level of detail required by various stakeholders, as documented in the communication plan. Common formats for performance report include Gantt charts, S-curves, histograms and tables.

ADMINISTRATIVE CLOSURE

The project or phase, after either achieving its objectives or being terminated for other reason, requires closure. Administrative closure consists of documenting project results to formalize acceptance of the project by the sponsor, or customer. It includes collecting project records, ensuring that they reflect final specifications; analyzing project success, effectiveness, and lessons learned; and archiving such information for future use.

Administrative closure activities should not be delayed until the project completion. Each phase of the project should be properly closed to ensure that important and useful information is not lost. In addition, employee skills in the data base should be updated to reflect new skills and proficiency increases.

TOOLS AND TECHNIQUES FOR ADMINISTRATIVE CLOSURE

1. Performance reporting tools and techniques
2. Project reports.
3. Project presentations.
4. Outputs from administrative closure

PROJECT REPORTING

Good project reporting will reduce the need for and length of meetings. According to Ghattas and McKee (2001), reporting serves several functions:

1. Informing stakeholders of project status and projections
2. Assisting team members in staying on track
3. Confirming action items as a result of agreements and changes
4. Supporting requests for changes in resources, time and or scope
5. Fulfilling contractual obligations
6. Keeping the flow of funding

The project manager and team will communicate with and report to project stakeholders as follows:

I. Monthly Status Report

Written monthly status and progress reports are to include:

- Work accomplished since the last reports.
- Work planned to be performed during the next reporting period.
- Deliverables submitted since the last report.
- Deliverables planned to be submitted during the next reporting period.
- Work tasks in progress and currently outside of expectations for scope, quality, schedule or costs.
- Risks identified and actions taken or proposed to migrate.
- Lessons learned.
- Summary statements for posting on the firm's web site.

II. Monthly Resource Reports

Written monthly resource reports are to include:

a). Financial Resources.

- Total funds allocated.
- Total funds expended to date
- Estimated expenditures for entire project to completion.

b). Human Resources.

List of all volunteer team members categorized by current involvement i.e. activeness (pre-active, inactive, resigned).

- Current number of active volunteer team members.
- Estimated number of volunteer team members needed for project completion.

III. Milestone and critical status reports

A milestone is a significant event in the project, usually completion of a major deliverable.

a). Milestone status reports are to include the same terms as the monthly status reports, summarized to cover an entire project phase/period since the last milestone report, or entire project to date.

Milestone Report Template

Project:

Date of Milestone meeting/discussion:

Deliverables due	Due date	R/A/G*	Action to take to bring deliverable or task back on schedule

* **R** = Red flags [off plan—describe in detail: quality, cost, time]

A = Amber [is almost off schedule or will definitely be off schedule NOTE: you may need to agree the precise definition before use]

G = Green flags [to plan or better—show savings]

b). Critical status report—focuses on work task outside of expectations and other information as requested by stakeholders or stipulated by the project manager.

IV. Progress Report

A progress report shows the current status of the project, usually in relation to the planned status. The frequency and contents of progress report number vary depending on the length of the projects and progress being made. The report is a control tool intended to show the discrepancies between where the project is and where the plan says it should be. A common form of progress uses two columns-one for planned time and expenditure and one for actual.

Any additional content will depend on the format adopted. Some organizations include, only the *"raw facts"* in the report, and use those as a basis for discussion regarding reasons for variances and action to be taken at a project review meeting.

Other organizations (particularly those involved in long, complex projects) produce more comprehensive progress reports, with more expansion and comments. The report should monitor progress towards key milestones.

Milestone Slip Chart

This is another way of monitoring progress that could be included in a progress report.

The milestone slip chart compares planned and actual progress towards project milestone. Planned progress is shown on the x-axis and actual progress on the y-axis of where actual progress is slower than planned progress, slippage has occurred.

V. Completion Report

A completion report summarizes the results of the project and includes client signature. On completion of the project, the project manager will produce the completion report. The main purpose of the completion report is to document and gain client–off for the end of the project. The report should include a summary of project outcome. The completion report should contain:

i)   *Project objectives and the outcomes achieved*
ii) *The final project budget showing expected and actual expenditure* (if an internal client is involved, this information may be sensitive—the report may include or amend the budget report)
iii) *A brief outline of time taken compared with the original schedule.*

The completion report will also include provision for any ***on-going issues*** that will need to be addressed after completion. Such issues will be related to the project, but not part of the project. If they are part of the project, then the project is not yet completed. An example of an ongoing issue would be a failure of some lighting points to go on after the entire system has been tested and approved.

Responsibilities and procedures relating to any such issues should be laid down in the report.

The manager may find it useful to distribute a provisional report and request feedback. This should ensure the version presented for client sign off at the completion. Meeting is acceptable to all parties.

Project Status Report Form

Project Title: *Software implementation* **To date:** 27th January 2011

OVERALL STATUS	Behind xx days	On target		Ahead— days
KEY MILESTONES				
		Plan		Action
Project scope and plans signed off				
Contract signed off				
Acceptance signed off				
Training plan signed off				
Businesses processes signed off				
User training complete 9on existing test system)				
Pilot system established				
Pilot system reviewed				
Go live date confirmed				
Go live				
IMPACT OF SLIPPAGES				
M/S	Details/planned remedial action			Date
KEY RISKS				

Ref	Description	Management actions				Date

KEY ISSUES

Ref	Description				Resolve by date	

FINANCIAL STATUS

KShs '000'	'a' Initial budget	'b' Current budget (including app'd changes'	'c' Actual spent to date	'd' R/cast to complete	'e' Variance	Reason
Capital						
Fixed						
Variable						
Ongoing						
Fixed						
Variable						
TOTAL						

Note: variance = (c + d)-b

Other comments (notable achievements / major changes / planned absences, etc)

Project manager: Sibuor Ger

Project supervisor: Kwach Rakido

Monthly Project Status Report

General Information:	
Agency name:	Date:
Contact Name:	Phone:
Project ID:	For the period beginning: and ending:
Name of the project:	
Project Start Date:	Current Phase:

Key Questions

1) Has the project scope of work changed? Yes/No

2) Will upcoming target dates be missed? Yes/No

3) Does the team have resource constraints? Yes/No

4) Are there issues that require management attention? Yes/No

If any of the above questions is answered "yes", please provide an explanation of the "yes" answer.

Key Milestones for the Overall Project revised on <date>:

Milestone	Original Date	Revised Date	Actual Date

Milestones Planned for this month and Accomplished this month:

Milestone	Original Date	Revised Date	Actual Date

Accomplishments Planned for this month and not completed:

Milestone/Item/Accomplishment	Original Date	Revised Date
1)		
2)		
3)		
4)		

For each item listed above, provide a corresponding explanation of the effect of this missed item on other target dates and provide the plan to recover from this missed item.

Items Planned for Next Month:

Milestone	Original Date	Revised Date

(Use a chart like the following to show actual expenditures compared to planned levels. Break the costs into other categories as appropriate.)

Year-to-Date Costs (000)				
Fiscal Year 20__	Actual Costs to Date	Estimate to Complete	Total Estimated Costs	Total Planned Budget
Personnel Services				
Prof. and Outside Service				
Other Expenditures *				
Total Costs				

(Use a chart like the following if this project spans more than one fiscal year.)

Year-to-Date Costs (000)				
Grand Total For Project	Actual Costs to Date	Estimate to Complete	Total Estimated Costs	Total Planned Budget
Personnel Services				
Prof. and Outside Service				
Other Expenditures *				
Total Costs				

* Other Expenditures include hardware, software, travel, training, support, etc.

Attach the current risk list.

Attach the current issues/action item list (for the significant items that need management attention)

Glossary

Most Relevant Terms
Related To Evaluation and Controlling

Accountability—Obligation to demonstrate that work has been conducted in compliance with agreed rules and standards or to report fairly and accurately on performance results vis a vis mandated roles and/or plans

- *Ex: a report to parliament, to a board or a constituency.*
- *a* "summative evaluation" that can serve as an instrument hitherto.

Appraisal—overall assessment of the relevance, feasibility and potential sustainability of a programme/project prior to decision of funding.

- *Ex: a document of its merits and risks, submitted for approval in principle.*
- Assessment; ex ante evaluation is considered as a synonym.

AUDIT—independent or internal objective assessment of either compliance with applicable standards, criteria. statutes and regulations ("regularity audit") or the relevance, economy, efficiency, effectiveness ("performance audit")

- *Ex: a report*
- Inspection, regularity audit   verification; performance audit
  evaluation

Beneficiaries—the individuals, groups, or organizations, whether targeted or not, that ultimately benefit, directly or indirectly, from a programme/project

- *Ex: the communities benefiting from a public health programme*
- Outreach; target group (that is equal to or smaller than the beneficiary group)

Baseline data—data that describe the situation to be addressed by a programme or project and that serve as the starting point for measuring the performance of that programme or project.

Benchmark—reference point or standard against which progress or achievements may be compared, e.g., what has been achieved in the past, what other comparable organizations such as development partners are achieving, what was targeted or budgeted for, what could reasonably have been achieved in the circumstances.

Capacity development—the process by which individuals, organizations, institutions and societies develop their abilities individually and collectively to perform functions, solve problems and set and achieve objectives.

Cluster evaluation—an evaluation of a set of related projects and/or programmes.

Conclusion—a reasoned judgment based on a synthesis of empirical findings or factual statements corresponding to a specific circumstance. Example: The research and development programme of the Agricultural

Science and Technology Institute is strong in its technical aspects but weak in its linkage with target groups (see "Finding" for the difference between a conclusion and a finding).

Consistency

Compliance with the policies, guidelines, priorities, approaches set by an institution (UNDP, partner government . . .)

- Coherence
- Does our programme/project fit within the sector related policy?

Controlling

Key function within an organization consisting in selecting relevant data with respect to steering and reflecting its own performance, then analyzing, interpreting those data, with the aim to provide a robust basis for management decisions

Monitoring that limits itself to the mere observation of processes and results as shown by themselves or through indicators, while controlling goes a step further and includes the analysis and interpretation of data.

Direct beneficiaries—usually institutions and/or individuals who are the direct recipients of technical cooperation aimed at strengthening their capacity to undertake development tasks that are directed at specific target groups. In micro-level interventions, the direct beneficiaries and the target groups are the same.

Effectiveness—the extent to which a programme or project achieves its immediate objectives or produces its desired outcomes.

Did we achieve our objectives? To what extent did our outputs produce the desired outcomes?

Confine "efficacy" to: "achievement of objectives"

Efficiency—the optimal transformation of inputs into outputs.

Are we doing things right, in a proper and economically sound manner? assessment, review

Do we do the right things? Do we do things the right way?

Evaluation—a time-bound exercise that attempts to assess systematically and objectively the relevance, performance and success of ongoing and completed programmes and projects.

Feedback—as a process, consists of the organization and packaging in appropriate form of relevant information from monitoring and evaluation activities, the dissemination of that information to target users, and, most important, the use of the information as a basis for decision-making and the promotion of learning in an organization. Feedback as a product refers to information that is generated through monitoring and evaluation and transmitted to parties for whom it is relevant and useful. It may include findings, conclusions, recommendations and lessons from experience.

Finding—factual statement about the programme or project based on empirical evidence gathered through monitoring and evaluation activities. Example: Although its initial tests of the new technology for preventing soil erosion have been positive, the Agricultural Science and Technology Institute effort has generated only a lukewarm response from the target group of farmers, who are misinformed about the cost implications of that technology. (See "Conclusion" for the difference between a finding and a conclusion).

Goal (development objective)—the higher-order objective to which a development intervention is intended to contribute ; aim; development objective, overall objective, (at the level of desired impact)

Impact—see "Results"—positive and negative, primary and secondary long-term changes / effects produced by a programme/project, directly or indirectly, intended or unintended.

Ex: higher standard of living, increased food security, democratic rule of law: influences on the context, societal or physical environment

Indicator—Quantitative or qualitative factor or variable that provides a simple and reliable means to measure achievement, results, and to reflect processes as well as changes in the context.

Ex: increase in savings as an indicator of confidence in economic perspective and of trust in banking system; a sky with red fringe at dawn ; bad weather at noon.

Where can we measure the "temperature" of our activities; where should we read signals of expected changes?

Input—a means mobilized for the conduct of programme or project activities, i.e., financial, human and physical and material resources; means invested, time, money, energy, know-how

Lesson learned—learning from experience that is applicable to a generic situation rather than to a specific circumstance. Example: A strong information centre is essential to an institution dealing with research and development (R&D) as a channel for disseminating the results of its research programme to target groups and generating feedback from target groups on the usefulness of its R&D results.

Log frame

Management tool used to enhance the design of project /programme. It involves identifying strategic elements (goal, purpose, planned outputs, planned activities and inputs), delineating their causal relationships, specifying indicators as well as identifying the assumptions (influence or risks) that may influence success and failure.

It may facilitate planning, implementation and evaluation of programme/project, in a participatory and transparent manner; Logical Framework Approach, Project Framework

Monitoring—a continuous function that aims primarily to provide programme or project management and the main stakeholders of an ongoing programme or project with early indications of progress or lack thereof in the achievement of programme or project objectives.

Ex: set of information collected by a sailor; cockpit board or dashboard; follow up, controlling

Objective—purpose or goal representing the desired result that a programme or project seeks to achieve. A development objective is a long-term goal that a programme or project aims to achieve in synergy with other development interventions. An immediate objective is a short-term purpose of a programme or project.

Should be "smart", that means: **s**imple, **m**easurable, **a**chievable, **r**ealistic, **t**ime bound purpose; expected outcome ; **Outcomes**—see "Results".

Results of a programme/project relative to its objectives that are generated by its respective partners' outputs.

Ex: improved capacity of an institution to manage set and enforce policies; results, effects at purpose level

Outputs—see "Results".

The tangible products (goods, services) of a programme or project

Ex: extension services provided to rice farmers, advisory services delivered to an organization; project deliveries

Partner—organizations, institutions that collaborate to achieve mutually agreed upon objectives and share responsibility and accountability, benefits as well as risks and endeavours.

Performance—the extent to which a programme or project is implemented in an effective, efficient and timely manner.

Planning—the process through which goals and objectives of a programme/project are set, partners identified, inputs figured out, activities specified and scheduled, monitoring mechanisms defined, so that expected outputs and outcomes might be achieved in a timely manner.

Programme—a time-bound intervention that differs from a project in that it usually cuts across sectors, themes and/or geographic areas, involves more institutions than a project, and may be supported by different funding sources.

Programme approach—the process of defining and providing technical cooperation through a cohesive national programme framework, which in turn consists of a coherent set of interrelated policies, strategies, activities and investments designed to achieve a specific, national development objective.

Programme // Project Cycle Management ((PCM//PEMT))—the process to steer and manage all steps, starting from identification till completion, through appraisal, planning, implementation, monitoring, feedback and evaluation.

"PEMT" (Planning, Evaluation, Monitoring, and Transference into Action) is the interpretation of PCM that stresses process approach, partners' participation as well as human and institutional development related aspects.

Project—a time-bound intervention that consists of a set of planned, interrelated activities aimed at achieving defined objectives.

Project document—a document that explains in detail the context, objectives, expected results, inputs, risks and budget of a project supported by a donor.

Purpose—The publicly stated objectives of the development programme or project. Programme/project objectives; planned outcomes

Rating system—an instrument for forming and validating a judgement on the relevance, performance and success of a programme or project through the use of a scale with numeric, alphabetic and/or descriptive codes.

Recommendation—proposal for action to be taken in a specific circumstance, including the parties responsible for that action. Example: As a strategy to ensure the acceptability of its research results by target users, the Agricultural Science and Technology Institute should establish a centre for sharing of information between the target users and the Institute. Through a systematic information exchange programme, the Institute should provide target users with information on new technologies being developed and obtain their views on how to improve such technologies.

Relevance—the degree to which the objectives of a programme or project remain valid and pertinent as originally planned or as subsequently modified owing to changing circumstances within the immediate context and external environment of that programme or project.

Or relevance may imply the extent to which the objectives of a programme/project are consistent with beneficiaries' needs, country needs, and global priorities.

Significance; pertinence to what extent do we do the right things? Does it make sense?

Results—a broad term used to refer to the effects of a programme or project. The terms "outputs", "outcomes" and "impact" describe more precisely the different types of results.

Review—an assessment of the performance of a programme/project, periodically or on a ad hoc basis, triggered by management or a stakeholder

Evaluation, although frequently "evaluation" is used for a more comprehensive and/or more in-depth assessment than "review".

Reviews tend to emphasize operational aspects.

Stakeholders—groups that have a role and interest in the objectives and implementation of a programme or project; they include target groups, direct beneficiaries, those responsible for ensuring that the results are produced as planned, and those that are accountable for the resources that they provide to that programme or project (cf. "Target groups" and "Direct beneficiaries").

Strategic evaluation—an evaluation of a particular issue where timing is especially important owing to the urgency of the issue which poses high risks to, and has generated widely conflicting views from, stakeholders. It aims to advance a deeper understanding of the issue, reduce the range of uncertainties associated with the different options for addressing it, and help to reach an acceptable working agreement among the parties concerned.

Success—favorable programme or project result that is assessed in terms of effectiveness, impact, sustainability, and contribution to capacity development.

Sustainability—durability of positive programme or project results after the termination of the technical cooperation channeled through that programme or project;

static sustainability—the continuous flow of the same benefits, set in motion by the completed programme or project, to the same target groups; dynamic sustainability—the use or adaptation of programme or project results to a different context or changing environment by the original target groups and/or other groups.

Ex: a micro-credit scheme that is generating enough money for the scheme to operate, cover risks and develop its staff; durability, viability

Target groups—the main stakeholders of a programme or project that are expected to gain from the results of that programme or project; sectors of the population that a programme or project aims to reach in order to address their needs based on gender considerations and their socio-economic characteristics

APPENDICES

Appendix A

Best Practices and Recommendations for Monitoring and Evaluation in Development Projects / Programmes

Monitoring and Evaluation in the Context of Project Planning and Re-Planning

- The design of an effective and efficient M+E system requires a periodic review and if necessary refinement of the project strategy which is based on a transparent and consistent development hypothesis.
- M&E has to be based on clearly defined and specified indicators and milestones
- In order to define indicators for intended outcomes and impacts of a project, the different perspectives of various stakeholders have to be taken into account.
- It has proven to be helpful to imagine the future improved situation from the point of view of different beneficiaries.
- Indicators should be formulated predominately for those results for which an influence of project interventions can be attributed with convincing plausibility.
- Often quantitative and qualitative targets have to be set in an iterative manner based either on available data or on special base-line surveys.

- During the project planning phase the flows of M&E information (type, sender / receiver, time / frequency, form) and a schedule for specific M&E activities (e.g. reviews, surveys and planning events) have to be determined.
- Costs for M&E activities have to be considered, practical experience shows that 5-10% of the project budget are realistic and sufficient.

Implementation of a M&E *System*

- In order to ensure an efficient and effective implementation of M&E, a clear commitment by management and decision makers is essential.
- Staff has to be conversant and competent with the concept of M&E and its procedures, corresponding training has to be provided.
- Stakeholders—particularly beneficiaries—have to be linked to the M&E system through their involvement in data collection analysis and assessment as well as through feedback mechanisms.
- However, it must be kept in mind that participation of stakeholders also implies a cost to them.
- Therefore, beneficiaries should be involved to the extent they are affected and according to their potential to utilize monitoring information.
- Data collection has to be focused to the needs of management and stakeholders. Excessive data collection which can often be found in project M&E has to be avoided
- For data collection appropriate and standardized procedures have to be used (frequency, sources of data, means of data collection, responsibilities). Taking into account project activities, types of services and planned impacts.
- Available data from various sources should be used to the extent possible in order to avoid duplication and waste of resources.

- M&E results will be useful for decision making and management only, if communicated through clear, brief and focused reports.
- Information feed back for beneficiaries is essential but has to be tailored to their specific concerns and capacities.
- M&E must not be limited to the planned targets of the project but should also be sensitive to external factors and risks. However, experiences shows that project M&E can fulfil this only in a limited and restrictive manner.

Institutionalizing Monitoring and Evaluation

- In order to ensure the sustainability of M&E the system has to be institutionalized within the respective organisation(s). Through such an institutionalization the M&E activities are adopted and developed to a routine procedure in the system.
- Institutionalization means on the one hand a standardization of M&E procedures for various projects within one organisation. On the other hand it requires an integration of M&E into the procedures of different organisations or donors which steer / fund the project.
- Support networking for exchange of M&E information amongst different institutions.
- Information flows and reporting procedures must be considered and reflected in the design of the M&E system.
- For institutionalizing a project M&E within an organisation it is advisable to:
    - take the existing practices as a starting point
    - assign clear roles and responsibilities which reflect the central importance of M&E
    - consider cost implications and minimize additional resources required
    - Make M&E a regular function of staff by including M&E tasks into their ToR.

- Institutionalising M&E within an organisation normally requires advocacy at the levels of
  - ◦ top management e.g. by presenting best M&E practices from other organizations or projects, in order get their support and sufficient resources
  - ◦ middle management, e.g. through capacity building measures and sharing information with other institutions in order to support the effective implementation of M&E
  - ◦ Technical staff, e.g. through training and incentive systems.

Appendix B

Methods and Tools
for Monitoring and evaluation

Methods.	Tools.
Surveys	
Formal	Questioner's
Informal	Checklist.
Field days.	Terms of reference
Tours.	Open ended discussion.
Meetings	Data sheet.
On-spot—checks	Graphs.
Random checks	Seasonal calendars.
Reports.	Bar, pie, line scatter.

Business: Tools for monitoring effectiveness

(Economic change)

1) Increased employment.
2) Increased income.
3) Consumer benefits.

4) Links with other businesses.
5) Availability of goods and services.
6) Ecological effects.

Social Indicators

Indicators	Tools
1) Change in the individual attitudes, skills, work with others.	1) Process documentation, role analysis, work sheet, time use studied.
2) Change in role relation.	2) Role analysis, work-sheet, critical individual analysis
3) New opportunities.	3) List of contacts
4) Wider distribution of benefits.	4) Wealth index.
5) Ability to work together as a group.	
6) Influence on systems that cause poverty.	

Monitoring social costs. : Indicators for monitoring NGO effectiveness

1. Political linkages and policy changes.
2. Program outreach and selection of appropriate clients.

3. Management of credit program.
4. Effectiveness of technical assistance
5. Effectiveness of training programs.
6. Cost effectiveness of programs.
7. Sustainability of program.
8. Organizational growth.
9. Human qualities.

REFERENCES

Appleton, S. (1996) *"Problems in Measuring Changes in Poverty over Time,"* IDS Bulletin Vol. 27 No 1, Brighton, UK: Institute for Development Studies.

Balzer, G., Dimalanta, A. and Kunz W. (2004) InWent Second Training on Monitoring and Evaluation in Development Projects / Programmes 30th October-4th Nov 2004 Feldafing. Germany

Bamberger, M. and Hewitt, E.(1986) *Monitoring and Evaluating Urban Development Programs, A Handbook for Program Managers and Researchers.* World Bank Technical Paper no 53. (Washington, D.C.:

Buzzard, S. and Edgcomb, E. (1987) Eds. *Monitoring and Evaluating Small Business Projects for Private Development Organizations.* Private agencies collaborating together. (PACT) Washington

Casley, Dennis J. and Krishna, K.1987) *Project Monitoring and Evaluation in Agriculture.* Washington, D.C.: World Bank.

DAC/OECD (http://www.oecd.org/dac)

Ghattas, R.G. and McKee, L. S. (2002) *Practical Project Management.* New Jersey: Prentice-Hall

Hammond, A.A. Adrianne, E. Rodenburg, D. Bryant and Woodward, .R. (1995). Environmental Indicators: A Systematic Approach to Monitoring and Reporting on Environmental Policy Performance in the Context of Sustainable Development, Washington, D.C. World Resource Institute.

IFAD (2002) *Practical Guide on Monitoring and Evaluation of Rural Development Projects*

International Fund for Agricultural Development. (IFAD) (2002). "A Guide for Project M&E: Managing for Impact in Rural Development." Rome: IFAD. Available at http://www.ifad.org/evaluation/ guide/

Jiggins, J. (1995). "Development impact assessment of aid ion non-western countries. Impact assessment. In Meyer, m. and Singh, n (2003). "Two approaches to evaluating the outcomes of development project.

Kezsbom, D.S., Donald, L. S., and K.A. Edward. (1989). *Dynamic Project Management*. NY: Wiley.

Kumar, K. ed. (1993). *Rapid Appraisal Methods.* World Bank. Washington, D.C. "Evaluation Feedback for Development"

Kusek, J. Z. &. Rist, R. C. (2004) Ten Steps to a Results—Based Monitoring and

Evaluation System: A Handbook for Development Practitioners

Washington, D.C. The International Bank for Reconstruction and Development / The World Bank

Kusek, J. Z. and Rist, R. C. (2001). *"Building a Performance—Based Monitoring and Evaluation System: The Challenges Facing Developing Countries." Evaluation Journal of Australasia.* 1(2): 14–23.

Lawrence, K. and Gordon, J. (2005). *Project management and project network techniques.*7th Ed. Prentice-Hall. Maylor, Haevey (1998). *Project Management.* Pitman

Leeuw, F. L. (2003). "Evaluation of Development Agencies' Performance: The Role of Meta-Evaluations." Paper prepared for the Fifth Biennial World Bank Conference on Evaluation and Development. Washington, D.C. July 15–16.

Lewis, J. (1997). *Team-Based Project Management.* New York: AMACOM

Lewis, J. (1998). *Mastering Project Management.* New York: McGraw-Hill,

Lewis, J. (2000). *The Project Manager's Desk Reference,* 2d ed. New York: McGraw-Hill,

Lewis, J. (2001). *Project Planning, Scheduling, and Control,* 3d Ed. New York: McGraw-Hill.

Meyer, M and Singh, N (2003). *"Two Approaches to Evaluating the Outcomes of Development Projects."* In Eade, Deborah (Ed). *Development Critical Reflections.* Oxfam.

OECD. (1999). *"Improving Evaluation Practices: Best Practice Guidelines for Evaluation and Background Paper"*

Operations Evaluation Department, World Bank (1994). *"Building Evaluation Capacity",* Lessons and Practices No. 4, November

Patton, M.Q. (1997). *"Utilization—Focused Evaluation—The New Century Text".* 3rd Edition, Sage Publications,

Pinto, K. J. ((2008). Project Management: Achieving Competitive Advantage. New Jersey: Prentice-Hall

Project Management Body of Knowledge (PMBOK—2001). Project management guide book. www.pmi.org

Project Management Institute (1996.) *A Guide to Project Management Body of Knowledge,* Upper Darby: PA: PMI.

Scriven, M. (1991). "*Evaluation Thesaurus, Fourth Edition.*" Sage Publications.

Singh, D. K. and Nyandemo, S.M. (2004). *Aspects of Project Planning, Evaluation and Implementation.* Dehra Dun—India: Singh Bishen

Shtub, A., Bard, J.F., and Globerson, S. (2005). *Project Management: Process, Methodologies & Economics.*2nd Ed. New Jersey: Prentice-Hall

Swiss Agency for Development and Co-operation SDC (2002) *Evaluation and Controlling Unit* (http://www.sdc.admin.ch)

UNDP (2002).*Handbook on Monitoring and Evaluating for Results.* New York: UNDP Evaluation Office.

UNDP. (2001). "*Results-oriented Monitoring and Evaluation—A Handbook for Programme Manager.*" Office of Evaluation and Strategic Planning

UNDP (September 1993). *Office of the Administrator, Division for Audit and Management Review, Organization Handbook.*

UNICEF (1991). "*EVALUATION—A UNICEF Guide for Monitoring and Evaluation—Making a Difference?*" Evaluation Office.

USAID. (1998). *"Managing for Results at USAID"*, presentation prepared by Annette Binnendijk for the Workshop on Performance Management and Evaluation, New York, 5-7 October.

World Bank (1995). *"Monitoring and Evaluation Plans in Staff Appraisal Reports in fiscal year 1995"*. Report No. 15222, December